BEARS

BEARS
WITHOUT FEAR

KEVIN VAN TIGHEM

RMB

Rocky Mountain Books
www.rmbooks.com

Library and Archives Canada Cataloguing in Publication

Van Tighem, Kevin, 1952-
     Bears : without fear / Kevin Van Tighem.

Includes bibliographical references and index.
Also issued in electronic format.
ISBN 978-1-927330-57-9 (HTML).—ISBN 978-1-927330-58-6 (PDF)
ISBN 978-1-927330-31-9 (pbk.)

     1. Bears—Canada, Western. 2. Human-bear encounters—Canada, Western.
I. Title.

QL737.C27V363 2013   599.7809712   C2013-900445-9

Front cover photo: *Front view of Female Brown Bear, 8 years old, walking*
Eric Isselée

Printed in China

Rocky Mountain Books acknowledges the financial support for its publishing program from the Government of Canada through the Canada Book Fund (CBF) and the Canada Council for the Arts, and from the province of British Columbia through the British Columbia Arts Council and the Book Publishing Tax Credit.

 Canadian Heritage Patrimoine canadien   Canada Council for the Arts Conseil des Arts du Canada

 BRITISH COLUMBIA ARTS COUNCIL
Supported by the Province of British Columbia

This book was produced using FSC®-certified, acid-free paper, processed chlorine free and printed with soya-based inks.

CONTENTS

PREFACE

My first bear was probably at the old Banff garbage dump during a holiday with my parents sometime in the early 1960s. My family, like many others in those days, liked to watch black bears scramble about in piles of refuse – it was a highlight of any park visit. As a member of a family of anglers and hunters, and later as a wilderness hiker and biologist, I've been around bears one way or another ever since.

I thought I knew bears, and was smug in my own comfortable attitude toward them, until the summer and fall of 1983. I worked that year on a wildlife inventory of two rugged national parks in British Columbia: Mount Revelstoke and Glacier. A colleague returned early one day from his fieldwork after a black bear had chased him up a tree. This was in the days before pepper-based bear sprays were available. I ribbed him about letting a mere black bear cow him and later went out to the site to complete the sampling he'd left unfinished.

Deep into a dense aspen forest I paused, suddenly aware of a prickling tension in the air. A large male black bear was watching me, about thirty metres away. No cause for concern. I raised my arms high to make myself look as large as possible, and yelled at him. It had always worked before. But this bear lowered his head, half-turned toward me and fixed me with a cold, hostile stare.

My legs went rubber. Cockiness gave way to helpless fear. Even as I looked around for a safe retreat, I knew in the back of my mind that I had behaved like a boor, invading the bear's peace and privacy with my loud and aggressive behaviour. Weak with fear, I eased quietly away through the trees. The bear, mercifully, simply watched me go.

A week later, a helicopter deposited Gail and me on the brushy floodplain of the remote Incomappleux River for more fieldwork. As we set up camp, I spotted a small grizzly about to cross the river toward us. I shouted and waved my arms to get the bear's attention. When it finally saw me, it retreated back up the hill.

At daybreak the next morning, I encountered yet another bear. I could hear it moving about uphill in dense avalanche alder, so I shouted and whistled to let it know I was there. No doubt curious about the strange sounds, the bear promptly sneaked closer to investigate. Hearing a faint rustling of twigs, I crouched to look beneath the alders and came face to face with a startled grizzly. Within seconds, I was five metres up a lone spruce tree and the bear, no doubt as shocked as I was, had vanished.

Next day: yet another grizzly encounter. Gail had headed out with the helicopter after the pilot dropped me high in an alpine basin, alone. No sooner had I picked out a campsite than I noticed movement out of the corner of my eye and spotted a very large grizzly picking his way across the mountain slope above me. Reaching a gully full of old snow, the bear sat on his haunches and tobogganed down the slope, breaking into a trot at the bottom and emerging into the small meadow where I had left my food and supplies. Not knowing how else to keep him from stumbling on my cache, I shot some pen flares at him. The bear turned and fled down the avalanche path.

I slept poorly that night, alone in my small tent. In the morning, the mist-shrouded mountainside looked ominous. Too many chance encounters with bears over too short a time had eroded my easy confidence.

That September, I woke in the dark of an unforgettable night to the ring of the phone. My father's voice was almost unrecognizable. I felt the cold paralysis of fear clamp down on my heart as he struggled to tell me the news. He was calling from a hospital emergency ward: a grizzly had severely mauled my younger sister and her husband. They had been hiking in Waterton Lakes National Park and surprised the bear on a sheep carcass in a snow flurry.

This sort of thing isn't easy to write about. These many years later, I still struggle with the sense that somehow it should have been me, not her. Her injuries plagued her to the end of her days. Friends and family suffered with her.

That strange and disconcerting year took me from thinking about bears in a superficial, self-satisfied manner to trying to come to terms with what bears really are and how we might best live with them. I have watched, contemplated, read about and discussed bears many times since then. I have come to know a few bears as individuals; watched others try to coexist with humans only to die at their hands; struggled to break through my own human-centred biases and fears to a real understanding of these fascinating, intelligent and sometimes dangerous wild animals.

This book is a product of the effort.

ACKNOWLEDGEMENTS

Many people were willing to contribute their knowledge, skills and energies in order to make this book possible; I can't thank them enough. Bill Dolan, Rob Watt and my other colleagues kindly took on my work responsibilities for the months I took off to write the first edition. I had to retire in order to find time for this second edition.

Gail Van Tighem, my wife and favourite outdoors companion, has shared many of my bear experiences over the years. I'm grateful to her for those years, and for helping clarify both the thinking and the writing that went into these pages.

Much of the information in this book came from a great variety of individuals and published materials. Thanks go, in particular, to: Tom Beck, Arlene Bethune, Maureen Enns, Keith Everts, Craig Fager, Stephen Herrero, Eric Langshaw, Wayne McCrory, Cam McTavish, Steve Michel, Paul Paquet, Steve Pozzanghera, the late Andy Russell, Charlie Russell, Doug and Lynne Seus, David Spalding, Gordon Stenhouse, Beth Towe, Rob Watt, John Weaver and John Woods, as well as staff of various state and provincial wildlife agencies who responded promptly to information requests.

Gordon Stenhouse of the Foothills Research Institute kindly provided a detailed, critical view of this book in its entirety, as did Gail. Wayne McCrory reviewed the original text. I also appreciate the feedback of those who reviewed portions of this revised version: Maureen

A startled grizzly bear.

Enns, Peter Jowett, Cam McTavish, Paul Paquet and Charlie Russell.

To the extent that this book is thorough and accurate, it's due in large part to the generous help of these and others. On the other hand, I insist on full credit for any errors that survived the edits and reviews. And the opinions are my own; don't blame anyone else.

This book is dedicated to the bears and wild places of western North America, and to Gail's and my children – Corey, Katie and Brian – who grew up among them.

1
INTRODUCTION

Bears are bigger than we are – more powerful, more potent. They haunt the edges of the forests of our imagination. They grow larger than life as night approaches. Small children lie awake in the dark, listening for bears outside the tent. Their parents listen too.

Out there, bears are prowling the shadows. Overhead, the Great Bear stalks out of myth across a sea of stars.

Since the dawn of time, humans and bears have lived uneasily together, sharing the same foods and the same preferred habitats, avoiding one another as much as possible out of wariness and fear.

Almost every aboriginal culture has had its bear cult, a secret society reserved for the strongest, most dangerous warriors. Killing a bear has long been counted proof of the highest bravery. Skinned, a bear looks eerily human, adding to the supernatural mystique of the beast.

Fear of bears seems almost to be part of what it is to be human. Our species emerged out of the depths of time into a world already populated by these great carnivores. Before we mastered iron and later developed firearms, we had few defences against bears – only watchful caution and elaborate ceremonies and sacrifices to ward off fear.

Kootenae Appee, a Piikani war chief who sought to

A black bear forages for dandelions.

hinder the explorations of David Thompson two hundred years ago, was reported by Thompson to have said: "Before the white men came to us we were weak. Every year the grizzled bears destroyed many of us; our arrows were headed with stone which broke on them…"

Once we developed modern firearms, however, fear became a force for extirpation.

England no longer has bears – human fear killed them all long before Magna Carta was written. California once had thousands of grizzlies; now, none. Until only recently, there were no more black bears in the hills of Kentucky, where Davy Crockett was reputed to have killed his first at the age of three. Plains grizzlies no longer roam the breaks of the Saskatchewan and Missouri Rivers. Polar bears no longer forage along the banks of the lower St. Lawrence.

Where human populations grow, bears have traditionally dwindled or disappeared. But when we return to the wild, to places where bears still survive, all our primeval fears awaken again. The risk of an automobile accident on the way to bear country far outstrips the risk of a close-range encounter with a bear, but it's the bear that worries us as we hurtle down the pavement at a hundred kilometres an hour.

What are bears, that they frighten us so? How are we to live with them in a shrinking world?

Perhaps more to the point, how are they to live with us?

THE QUALITY OF MERCY

There was a time when humans had little defence against bears. Now, in most cases, bears have no defence against us. The sheer weight of human population growth

A mother grizzly and her cub digging up sweetvetch roots.

– seven billion and counting – and human ambitions leave precious little room for other dominant animals in the earth's beleaguered ecosystems.

Rancher-biologist Charlie Russell has studied bears at closer range and with greater sympathy than most other people. In his book *Spirit Bear*, Charlie describes many close encounters with the bears of BC's coastal rainforest – bears hunting for food – that passed without any aggressive behaviour on the part of the bear. The bears could have crushed him, but they didn't.

Many people describe encounters at close range with grizzly and black bears that – popular prejudice tells us – should have led to disaster. Instead, the bears usually fled or paid no attention. At worst, they might have shown a persistent sort of curiosity.

Most bear encounters end peacefully. The truth is that

bears usually have more to fear from a human encounter than humans have to fear from a bear encounter – our exaggerated sense of danger adds to the bear's risk.

One late June day in Waterton Lakes National Park, a decade after the bear attack that changed my sister's life forever, I stopped to check a roadside beaver pond that sometimes holds trout, in anticipation of the fishing season that would open soon. Having checked the pond in several places and found no fish, I took a shortcut back to the road through a grove of aspens.

Pushing my way through the fringe of saplings into the sudden shadows of the forest, I froze in mid-stride as the smell of wet fur engulfed me. Something stirred in the greenery carpeting the forest floor and then a little head appeared. A grizzly cub was foraging five metres to my left. A moment later, I saw its sibling, even closer.

My heart was suddenly pounding in my chest like a sledgehammer, the skin of my face tight with fear. Where was their mother?

Then I saw her, perhaps ten metres away, tearing at a cow parsnip. She raised her head, a green stem hanging from her mouth, and turned to face me. Our eyes met. I knew I was finished, that my wife and our small children were going to have to deal with the horror of my death. I was furious and ashamed of myself for having left the bear spray on the floor of the car when it would have been no trouble at all to bring it, even for what was meant to be a quick jaunt off the roadside.

I lowered my eyes from hers, shoulders slumped, now feeling chagrin more than fear. Worse than knowing I was about to die was the realization that it would be entirely my own fault.

The cubs fed on, scarcely aware of the man standing beside them. And then their mother, after a long, calm look, turned her back on me and pulled the top off another cow parsnip. Unbelievably, she had chosen to give me the benefit of the doubt.

I took a step back, then another, then eased out of the shadowed grove into the brilliant sunshine of what felt like a reborn world. Birds were singing. I was alive.

I hurried back to the car, amazed and deeply grateful for the gentle tolerance of a grizzly mother who had just turned my assumptions inside out.

That mother bear and her cubs died a short time later, after they got into an old wooden granary on a nearby ranch. A conservation officer live-trapped them and released them several hundred kilometres away from their home. Within a week, the radio collar he had placed on the mother went into mortality mode. One by one, the cubs' signals vanished too. Lost in a landscape of strange bears and unfamiliar human activities, it was predictable that the bear who spared my life would soon lose her own.

A Stoney Nakoda elder once told me that the bear is a teacher. Perhaps there is something we can yet learn from the quality of mercy in bears: the restraint and reserve they show us more often than not. We have arrived at a time in Earth's history when the future of bears and many other animals now depends on our ability to demonstrate those same qualities of mercy, restraint and reserve. That can only begin when we have learned to master our fear.

Learning to understand bears better would be a good start.

2

BEARS IN HUMAN CULTURE

NORTH AMERICA'S FIRST PEOPLES

Most of North America's First Peoples have traditionally viewed the bear as a being of great power – potentially a strong ally, sometimes a powerful adversary. Some hunt bears; others have taboos against killing bears except in self-defence. Among many First Nations, to kill a bear was once considered one of the greatest feats of bravery a hunter could perform, but it also required prayer and ceremony to avoid the wrath of the animal's dead spirit. Stone-tipped arrows, spears or atlatls were weak weapons for young men facing an animal as much as four times their weight. Tribes along the coasts of what are now British Columbia and Alaska often carved bear images into totems, reflecting high esteem.

The Nuu-chah-nulth, who have occupied the Pacific coast for millennia, have long recognized the potent spirituality in the bears with whom they share the coastal forests, salmon streams and salal tangles of their homeland. George Woodcock, in his book *Peoples of the Coast*, described the ceremonial honour accorded bears killed for their meat and hides. In the Nuu-chah-nulth village of Tahsis, hunters placed a bear they had killed

On a totem pole in Vancouver, the figure of a bear is positioned beneath a Thunderbird.

Honouring the dead

When Kwakwaka'wakw hunters killed a bear, they honoured the power of the animal with ceremonies before butchering the carcass. In one such ceremony, described by an early anthropologist, the hunter placed his hand against the paw of the fallen bear and recited a short prayer thanking the bear, as a friend, for making the hunt a success. The hunter then asked the bear to share its power of capturing salmon and other game.

in a sitting position facing the chief. They adorned it with the ceremonial headdress of a chief and dusted the dead guest with eagle's down. Only then did they skin and butcher the bear and cook its meat in a stew.

At the feast that followed, only a small number of people ate the bear stew because anyone who ate bear meat was then required to abstain from eating salmon for several weeks to avoid offending the fish.

EUROPEAN ATTITUDES TOWARD BEARS

The warrior people of northern Europe once viewed bears in much the same way as North American First Peoples did. They considered the bear alternately a gentle giant and a powerful and implacable foe. The bear was a totemic animal that could give chosen individuals great powers in war and leadership. Killing a bear, eating its heart or donning its hide, they believed, could give men bear-like qualities.

In a commentary on a collection of German folklore, Donald Ward writes that hunting cultures believed people turned into animals when they wore animal skins.

They also believed that "predators have essentially human cores. It is thought that should they choose to walk around as humans, they would only need to shed their animal skins. Conversely, a human donning an animal skin ... can actually become, in his mind, the animal." Both these ancient beliefs gave rise to legends of were-animals.

Certain great warriors were famous for working themselves into frenzies in battle, convinced that they had the strength and fury of bears. The Vikings and some northern German tribes called such warriors "berserkers," from *ber* (bear) and *serkr* (coat). The English word "berserk" comes from the same root.

J.R.R. Tolkien, who specialized in the study of ancient European languages, drew the plot of his famous fantasy novel *The Hobbit* from the mythologies and folk tales of Europe. He based one of his characters, Beorn, on the berserker tradition. Tolkien writes: "... you must be careful not to annoy him, or heaven knows what will happen. He can be appalling when he is angry, though he is kind enough if humoured. Still, I warn you he gets angry easily.... He is a skin-changer. He changes his skin; sometimes he is a huge black bear, sometimes he is a great strong black-haired man with huge arms and a great beard."

The nations tamed under the Roman Empire, however, had a different relationship with bears. They were obsessed with imposing human order and control and nature. For them, bears represented nature's power and savagery. Aristocrats in these societies often sponsored public displays involving the torture of bears, perhaps to demonstrate man's dominance over nature. Histories say the Roman emperor Gordian liked to watch bloody matches pitting bears against dogs or gladiators. He watched the deaths of close to a thousand bears. The attraction of bear-baiting persisted for centuries; England's Queen Elizabeth I reportedly enjoyed the sight of thirteen bears being torn apart by dogs.

Bears of the star fields

The Big Dipper, one of the first constellations children learn to identify, forms part of a larger constellation called Ursa Major, which is Latin for "great bear."

Ursa Major gets its name from a Greek myth about Zeus and one of his many infidelities. Zeus was married to Hera, but fell in love with Callisto. When Hera learned of the affair, she swore vengeance, so Zeus turned Callisto into a bear to disguise her from his furious wife.

Looking like a bear, however, carries its own risks. One day Callisto's own son, Arcas, saw a bear while hunting and, unaware that it was his own mother, raised his spear to kill it. To protect Callisto, Zeus changed Arcas into a bear cub. Then, to head off future disasters, he put both bears among the stars. Hera saw this and finally got her revenge: she decreed that both bears would never rest again and doomed them to rotate endlessly around the night sky.

Finnish tradition holds that the bear lives in the sky with his family – the stars in the Big Dipper are Otava and his brothers.

The Big Dipper is associated with bear in some of the mythologies of North America's First Peoples. The Kainai, for example, have a story of a young woman who was caught mating with a bear in the forest. Her

Ursa Major as depicted in a painting by Dan Hudson.

brothers killed the bear, leaving their sister to mourn her lost lover. She cut off his paws to remember him and returned home only to face taunting and humiliation. Finally, upset beyond endurance, she roared in such anger that she became a bear.

When her brothers returned from hunting they learned what had happened and fled. Their sister pursued them. Eventually she caught up and drove them up a tree.

The bear-woman shook the tree until her brothers began to lose their grip. One of her brothers managed to shoot her with an arrow. Dead, she turned back into the sister they remembered and, filled with remorse, the brothers agreed that they deserved exile. The powerful brother then shot an arrow into the sky and they followed it up. They became the Seven Brothers – the same seven stars that we know today as the Big Dipper.

The symbolic subjugation of nature to civilized man took other forms too. Europeans commonly trained chained bears to perform as clowns. Reducing a powerful animal to a silly-looking entertainer was just as destructive of wild bears as bear-baiting.

When Europeans arrived in North America, they brought their ambivalent attitudes toward bears with them. As the newcomers set about taming the new continent the abundant black bears they encountered were curious, sometimes entertaining and occasionally destructive. Bears, like nature itself, were tolerated only to the extent that they provided amusement; after that the project of civilizing a new world demanded that they be killed.

Werebears

Finns and Laplanders had many stories of shape-changers – mostly werebears and a few werewolves. One common theme involves a woman whose husband sometimes took the shape of a bear. One evening, when the man knew he was soon to become a bear, he grew worried for her safety. Saying he would have to leave her for a while, he warned her that she should watch out because she might be attacked by a dangerous bear. Sure enough, that night a huge bear attacked her but she was ready and escaped to safety. Later she learned the truth about the bear. Once she knew the truth, the spell no longer worked and her husband was freed of the curse.

Bears are commonly represented on totem poles.

"On a stormy day in the middle of an unusually severe winter, a black bear, hungry, no doubt, and seeking something to eat, came strolling down through our neighborhood from the northern pine woods. None had been seen here before, and it caused no little excitement and alarm, for the European settlers imagined that these poor, timid, bashful bears were as dangerous as man-eating lions and tigers, and that they would pursue any human being that came in their way."
—John Muir, Wisconsin, 1850s (from *The Story of My Boyhood and Youth*)

BEARS IN MODERN CULTURE

Bears are everywhere and nowhere in modern culture. At a time in history when the vast majority of North Americans live in places where they will never see real bears, bears of human conception abound in books, art, movies, the names of sports teams and countless consumer products.

Children grow up hugging teddy bears, listening to Winnie the Pooh stories and enjoying Yogi Bear cartoons on morning television. Teenagers watch movies such as *Grizzly* ("18 feet of gut-crunching terror!") or *The Bear*. Conservation groups auction bear paintings to raise funds. Investors worry about "bear markets" and gun-holster manufacturers promote their products as being "grizzly-tough."

For the most part, however, the bears with which we surround ourselves are little more than furry reflections of human fears, wishes or fond imaginings. The bears we buy, sell and invent rarely even come close to representing the real living creatures whose names they borrow.

North American culture has simplified the idea of bears into three dominant themes: the lovable clown, the marauding monster or the besieged wilderness creature.

The lovable clown motif appears in Disney movies, Yogi and Boo-boo cartoons, Winnie the Pooh, Paddington stories and other children's literature. In the early days of North American tourism, parks and resorts promoted this image with feeding programs or strategically placed garbage dumps that lured in bears for the entertainment of middle-class tourists. The garbage-addicted bears were amusing at first, standing on their legs and waddling awkwardly to reach food, getting into flour or molasses and emerging smeared and clown-like. Inevitably, this treatment corrupted many bears to the point that they became aggressive and were then killed to protect the same tourists who remained blissfully unaware that their choice of entertainment had created the problem.

Bears are often unfairly represented as vicious predators.

The second common representation of bears – as marauding monsters – likely arose as much from the aggressive depredations of such spoiled bears as it did from the frontier myth of the killer grizzly. "At the turn of the [twentieth] century and for the next thirty or forty years," says wildlife artist Maureen Enns, "we saw the animal as a dangerous part of the landscape. We always saw the bear portrayed with claws extended, mouth open." That image appears often in the works of Frederic Remington, Charlie Russell and other frontier painters. It's no less common in written literature, from western cowboy novels to Ernest Thompson Seton's *The Biography of a Grizzly*. Prevalent even today in taxidermy and some works of sculpture, the marauding monster motif comes out of the fears and insecurities of men confronted by wild landscapes that they did not understand and that magnified their sense of vulnerability. In the mythology of the Old West, all rivers were torrents, all grizzlies man-eaters, and all native people savages. The frontier ethos called for damming rivers, killing bears and subjugating "Indians": transferring the violence of the newcomers' own fears onto the objects of those fears. Today the marauding bear survives mostly in horror stories and B-movies like the eminently forgettable *Grizzly*, where a rampaging six-metre grizzly bear fights helicopters and eats pretty women.

James Oliver Curwood's frontier classic, *The Grizzly King*, was the basis for the 1988 movie *The Bear*. A trained Kodiak bear named Bart stars as a grizzly who adopts an orphaned black bear cub and fights to protect him when a guide and his hunter invade their wilderness refuge. The book and the movie represent the third popular bear motif: fascinating but ultimately doomed wilderness creature. In the realm of non-fiction, Andy Russell's *Grizzly Country* represents a powerful version of this idea.

But in serving as icons for human superiority over lesser creatures (the friendly clown), our fears of wild nature (the marauding monster) or our nostalgia for paradise lost (beleaguered wilderness creature), the bears that populate modern North American culture bear little resemblance to the real animal. Sentimentalized, politicized, demonized ... bears live out their lives as real bears, quietly unaware of the fog of constructed meanings that surrounds them and, too often, determines their fate in a world they must share with ever-increasing numbers of people.

Maureen Enns discovered this when she embarked on a multi-year project to paint, film and write about the grizzlies of Banff National Park as "monarchs of the wilderness." She started from the premise that grizzly bears symbolize North America's dwindling wildness: dangerous creatures doomed to flee from or fight back against the incursions of modern man. As she spent more time in bear country, however, she found herself seeing a very different animal than the one she had thought she already knew. Her art and the bear converged into a lifetime adventure in learning to perceive the real grizzly that lives outside our heads

Enns's experience led her into a new kind of bear art that looks for the bear where it really lives, rather than in the popular prejudices of a society that has become, as one naturalist put it, "orphaned from nature."

Art and myth

A twelve-foot sculpture of Old Mose, the last known grizzly from the state's South Park area, towers over a gathering place called the Grizzly Courtyard in Alamosa, Colorado. Hunters admitted that the bear seemed more curious than aggressive when hounds finally cornered him in 1904, but the statue portrays him on his hind legs, claws extended and face distorted in a vicious growl.

Grizzly bear portrayals in western art usually reflect human fears of an animal more powerful than us. Western myths concentrate on legendary cattle killers like Old Ephraim, the last Utah grizzly, or famous Colorado stock killers like Mose, Bigfoot Mary and Clubfoot. Old Mose was rumoured to have killed three men and eight hundred head of cattle, making him a powerful emblem of the viciousness of bears.

Where written records survive, however, the violent encounters between man and grizzly that dominate western sculptures, paintings and legend take on a more poignant flavour. Cowboys or hunters actually triggered many grizzly attacks when they shot and wounded the bears on sight. Old Mose, for example, was full of healed-over bullet wounds when he finally died. Other attacks were by desperate mothers defending their doomed cubs.

Even the exploits of great stock killers were exaggerated. Many cows and sheep died from poisoning by toxic weeds, accidents, lightning and drought. When herders and cowboys found grizzlies scavenging the carcasses, the bears had no chance for a fair trial. Even today, too many westerners – never having seen a grizzly – accept as received wisdom the prejudiced view that grizzlies and people can't coexist.

Frontier art portrays a time of exceptional violence, frequent tragedy and occasional heroism. But those images take on new meaning as new generations strive to develop a culture worthy of the West we have inherited. The violence, after all, was mostly man-made – imposed by outsiders upon the West, its original peoples and its wildlife. Some of those bears, doomed to violent deaths through humans' ignorance and fear, may have been among the frontier era's true tragic heroes.

Teddy bears

Teddy bears originated when the popular US president Theodore Roosevelt made headlines in 1902 by refusing to kill a black bear. His hunting companions, concerned that the president hadn't had much luck, ran a black bear down with hounds. After a fierce struggle during which the bear killed one of the dogs, they chained the bear to a tree for Roosevelt to shoot. Roosevelt, an ardent conservationist who believed strongly in the principles of fair chase, indignantly refused to kill the helpless animal.

The *Washington Post* commemorated the president's action with a cartoon by Clifford Berryman that quickly became famous as an icon for sportsmanlike restraint. It caught the attention of Morris Michtom, a Brooklyn entrepreneur. Michtom's wife, Rose, had designed a toy bear, so Michtom wrote to the president and asked his permission to market the toy as "Teddy's bear."

Roosevelt wrote back, "I don't think my name will mean much to the bear business, but you're welcome to use it."

He was wrong. Teddy's bears caught on, and their range expanded rapidly to include the homes of virtually every small child in North America.

Roosevelt later became one of the founders of the Boone & Crockett Club, an organization that promotes sportsmanship and fair chase in hunting.

Bart

Movie stars that weigh over 1,400 pounds don't normally get starring roles. Bart, however, was an exception. Orphaned by a hunter in 1977, Bart lived out his life with animal trainers Doug and Lynne Seus in Heber Valley, Utah. Bart grew to be more than 9.5 feet tall and appeared in such movies as *The Bear*, *Legends of the Fall*, *The Clan of the Cave Bear*, *White Fang* and *The Edge*. He even appeared onstage at the 1998 Academy Awards. His most meaningful role, though, was as ambassador for s, an organization that raises funds to protect grizzly bear habitat in British Columbia, Idaho, Montana and Alaska.

When Bart died in 2000 at the age of twenty-three, Vital Ground's obituary noted that "because of Bart's life in captivity, many of his wild brothers and sisters are able to roam free."

www.vitalground.org

BEARS AND PARKS

Bears are fascinating animals, and many live in beautiful natural areas. Inevitably the world of the bear overlaps with the world of outdoor tourism, not least because some of those areas have been developed as national parks. A national park is a strange kind of hybrid beast in the world of land use – neither a strict nature reserve nor a resort, it blends the protection of nature and the promotion of tourism. The blending doesn't always work.

Banff, the first national park in all of Canada, exemplifies the complex conservation challenges that arise when bears and tourists share the same mountain landscapes. It also, however, shows the potential for a symbiotic, sustaining relationship between the two.

The Canadian government established Banff National Park in 1885 as a scenic tourist destination to help pay off the immense debt of a new coast-to-coast railway. Well more than a century later, the park has become the most heavily developed national park in North America. Its contradictions as a nationally treasured wilderness, continental transportation corridor and expensive tourism resort have spawned decades of controversy over the meaning of national parks.

A four-lane expressway and the Canadian Pacific main rail line slice through the Bow River valley – and some of the park's most productive bear habitat. Resort hotels, golf courses and townsites sprawl across the valley, displacing bears from feeding areas, blocking important wildlife travel corridors, and filling the woods with often naive tourists whose activities also lead to conflict with bears. Although the more remote parts of Banff National Park provide wilderness refuges, the critically important montane habitats of the Bow River valley were becoming increasingly uninhabitable by bears by the end of the twentieth century. For a bear, it had become easier to die in the Bow valley than to live there.

"Banff," said Harvey Locke, past president of the Canadian Parks and Wilderness Society, at the turn of the twenty-first century, "is a national disgrace."

As much as there was truth in Locke's assessment, however, it would be no less correct to say that Banff National Park's innovations in bear management have, more often than not, set new standards of practice for other parks and agencies in bear country.

In the middle years of the twentieth century, bears commonly foraged in national park garbage dumps and roamed campgrounds in search of human food. Tourists often threw food to bears foraging along roadsides. Crowds gathered at garbage dumps near Banff and Lake Louise to watch bears feeding on the refuse.

Valley-floor roads and trails, designed with no consideration for mountain ecology, led naive, poorly informed visitors into some of the best available bear habitat, displacing the warier bears from important natural food sources and setting up inevitable surprise encounters that often led to injuries or deaths – if not for the people involved, then for the bears.

Between 1970 and 1982, park wardens killed at least thirty-two grizzly bears in Banff National Park – an average of close to three per year. In 1980 alone, the body count was nine. Black bears, generally less valued by park authorities of the day, died at an even higher rate, but their lower profile meant their deaths were less well documented. Management action – death by warden – was by far the biggest single cause of unnatural bear deaths in Banff and other national parks.

In 1971 Parks Canada shut down the Lake Louise garbage dump and, ten years later, finally closed the dump near Banff. At the same time, it worked with private companies to develop new, bear-proof garbage bins that replaced the old "bear-feeder" garbage cans that had led so many bears to their first taste of trouble. Campground staff and park wardens began a new practice of confiscating food coolers or other temptations left out by sloppy campers and worked more aggressively to educate visitors about responsible behaviour in bear country.

The 1974 Parks Canada–commissioned National Film Board documentary *Bears and Man* delivered a powerful message about sharing wild country with bears. Park interpreters incorporated the movie into programs aimed at hikers, campers and others. It was a groundbreaking effort in bear education that retains its impact nearly half a century later.

All this effort paid off: during the twelve years from

The genealogy of Pooh

Alan A. Milne was a novelist, playwright and essayist who wrote frequently for the prestigious London-based magazine *Punch*. A friend of H.G. Wells, Milne was educated at Cambridge and in later years often expressed frustration that his reputation was based on his children's stories and not his adult writing.

Milne modelled the character of Christopher Robin on his own son, Christopher, who received his now-famous stuffed bear for his first birthday, on August 21, 1921. Milne's fictional Winnie the Pooh was actually a cross between the toy bear and a real one: young Christopher and his father frequently visited the real Winnie at the London Zoo.

Winnie, the real bear, was born not in England but somewhere near White River, Ontario. A young army officer named Harry Colebourn had got off the train there in August 1914 and met a hunter who had killed a black bear and captured her small female cub. Soon afterward, Colebourn, a veterinarian by training, bought the cub and took it with him when he shipped overseas to England with the 2nd Canadian Infantry Brigade.

Colebourn named the little bear Winnie after his own hometown of Winnipeg. Winnie soon became a familiar sight on Salisbury Plain, trailing after Colebourn and other soldiers and begging for food. The brigade adopted her as its mascot. When the soldiers shipped out for France in December, Colebourn had to make arrangements for the little bear's care. He lent her to the London Zoo, where he visited her often when he was on leave. He formally donated her to the zoo in 1918. Winnie became a popular attraction, entertaining thousands of British children before she died at the ripe old age of thirty.

The famous drawings of Pooh, however, depict a third bear: a toy belonging to Graham Shepard, the son of the illustrator. Hired by *Punch* in 1921, E.H. Shepard was one of the first illustrators to receive a share of book royalties – Milne insisted on giving him 20 per cent, in recognition of the role his drawings played in the success of Milne's books. Shepard also illustrated Kenneth Grahame's *The Wind in the Willows*.

1983 through 1994 only fifteen grizzlies died from management action. And in the first twelve years of the twenty-first century, park wardens had to kill only two. Destruction of so-called "problem bears" has now moved to the bottom of the list of ways in which bears in Banff die unnatural deaths.

Banff's problems, however, were more complicated than keeping bears away from food and garbage. As Canada's oldest national park, Banff has a development history that continues to make it difficult for bears to live normal lives in the mountain landscape.

The Trans-Canada Highway traverses the low-elevation Bow valley, through some of Banff's most diverse and productive wildlife habitats, from one side of the park to the other. By the late 1970s, the highway had become what biologists described as "a moving wall of steel" – its heavy traffic killed more than two hundred large animals a year, including bears. Growing traffic volumes were blocking animals trying to cross the valley.

Development was out of control too. The tourism industry – originally invited into the national park to help the park meet the needs of its visitors – had pretty much turned the tables on Parks Canada. Some business operators had adopted the arrogant view that the park existed primarily to serve their commercial ambitions and that if businesses wanted to expand, the bears should move. Parks Canada, lacking effective policy or regulatory tools to manage growth, approved more than a half billion dollars worth of private commercial development in little more than a decade. Each time the town of Banff, the village of Lake Louise, the three ski hills and a number of once-small bungalow camps expanded their footprints, bears lost valuable habitat and became exposed to increased conflict with humans.

By the late 1980s, development had virtually blocked the Bow River valley around the town of Banff, so that animals like bears and wolves were unable to move from one part of the park to another. The only beast doing well in the park was the tourism tiger that Parks Canada had by the tail.

Canada's national parks are meant for Canadians and their guests from other parts of the world to visit and experience. But Banff has come to exemplify a problem recognized as early as the 1920s by Canada's first commissioner of national parks, James Harkin, when he wrote: "It is the duty of those in charge (of parks) to make them freely accessible by road and trail, to permit, under regulation, for the private provision of accommodation, refreshments and other needs. But the more the parks are used, the more difficult it is to prevent abuse. There are increased demands for more roads, cheaper forms of amusement, commercial exploitation, and the danger is … the parks may lose the very thing that distinguished them from the outside world."

Banff, like all national parks, is protected from mining, logging and other forms of resource exploitation that have proven harmful to bear populations elsewhere. But tourism development is also a form of resource exploitation, one that Parks Canada has always had more difficulty controlling. This is likely due as much to historic ambivalence, which goes back to the very origin of Banff National Park as a hot springs resort, as it is to the tourism industry's economic and political influence. The problems had become so pronounced by the late 1990s that the Canadian government appointed two blue-ribbon expert panels to review the situation and advise on solutions.

The final recommendations of both the Banff–Bow Valley Study and the Panel on the Ecological Integrity of Canada's National Parks were as disconcerting as they were controversial. The reviews each confirmed that development had indeed gone too far. Banff's ecosystem was unravelling from too much development. But just as Parks Canada had mobilized earlier to close garbage dumps, install new, bear-proof garbage cans, educate park visitors about appropriate behaviour in bear country and enforce food and waste handling regulations, the organization set to work implementing the key recommendations.

Two decades later the Trans-Canada Highway is a four-lane divided expressway. Although highway expansion removed another wide swath of bear habitat from the park, a wildlife-barrier fence now encloses the highway from one side of the park to the other. Animal deaths have decreased to almost nothing. The barrier effect of the fenced highway has also been addressed with innovative wildlife crossing structures, ranging from narrow culverts under the highway to wide-span underpasses and massive overpass structures covered with trees and vegetation. Wildlife mitigation measures added many millions to the costs of the highway project, but they have proven effective at both reducing roadkills and restoring freedom of movement to wary animals like bears.

During the same two decades, Parks Canada removed a number of facilities from the Bow River valley, including a large cadet camp, a fenced bison paddock, a historic house, and ground facilities for aircraft at an emergency airstrip. While reducing the level of development helped restore wildlife movement corridors around the town of Banff, the imposition of permanent, legislated limits on both the town boundary and its commercial development also helped ensure that the gains wouldn't be offset by future expansion of the townsite. Outside the town, each bungalow camp also has a permanent limit on its size and footprint. No new ski area development is permitted until the ski area operator has signed on to a contractual agreement establishing permanent boundaries and skier capacity.

Banff National Park's innovations in garbage management and highway fencing and crossing structures set new standards for others in bear country. Towns like Canmore, Fernie and Golden have now adopted Banff's bear-proof garbage bins. Interstate highways in Montana, Utah and Colorado now install highway fencing and crossing structures as a matter of course.

Other agencies have widely adopted Banff's innovations in restoring bear habitat and minimizing conflict between bears and trail users. When Parks Canada began restoring fire to the mountain landscape through prescribed burning in the 1970s, it was widely perceived as an example of management lunacy. Banff had its share of learning experiences too, as when fires on the Sawback Range killed the trees they were meant to save or when, as happened inevitably in more than one instance, weather conditions changed and what were planned as small fires became huge. Today, however, the use of fire to restore bear habitat and add natural diversity to forested landscapes has become standard practice, not just in Banff but in national parks, provincial parks and even areas managed for forestry across the country.

Parks Canada continues to experiment with relocating trails out of Banff's valley-bottom bear habitats, seasonally closing important bear feeding areas to hikers or requiring hikers to travel in large groups, making bear spray mandatory in some areas, and improving sightlines along trails or near backcountry campsites by trimming bushes back. Where history has put popular campgrounds into forests containing abundant buffalo berry bushes, campground staff now routinely remove the female, berry-producing bushes to reduce the risk that hungry bears will be tempted to forage amid campers.

One of the least-known recent changes in bear management, however, may ultimately prove to be the most valuable.

For decades, Parks Canada had reduced the risk of deadly encounters between humans and bears by keeping humans and bears scared of one another. Park visitors faced a constant barrage of messages that all bears are dangerous. Bears got the same message about humans. Whenever a bear turned up close to campgrounds or roadsides, park wardens would haze it away with noisemakers or rubber bullets so that it would learn to associate humans with danger.

This approach was, in fact, fairly effective at reducing injuries and deaths. However, since most of the park's tourist facilities and roads are in the most productive bear habitats along valley floors, it has also had the effect of excluding bears from excellent feeding areas and keeping them constantly uneasy when around humans. In the same way, the messages of fear

Grizzly tracks on a Banff National Park trail.

have perpetuated the ambivalence most park visitors have about bears and discouraged others from even visiting the parks.

Charlie Russell has long been critical of this approach of harassing bears to keep people safe. "You know, it's an imposition, a great imposition to them to have to run every time a human shows up," he says. "These roadsides are productive areas and bears need productive land as much as we need those areas. It's kind of unfair of us to insist that they move off those places."

In the late 1990s, Parks Canada began moving in a different direction. Instead of telling tourists that bears were dangerous, leaving them in fearful ignorance, park staff put more emphasis on explaining how bears live and why they react in the ways they do to different kinds of human behaviour. The emphasis moved from promoting fear to promoting informed respect.

Instead of hazing bears away from roadsides, Parks Canada hired "bear guardians" to patrol roadsides. When bear guardians encounter a bear feeding peacefully near the road, they simply supervise the resulting bear jam and answer questions. This not only enables park visitors to enjoy unforgettable wildlife viewing experiences and learn about bears, it lets bears spend more time feeding rather than wasting time and energy fleeing to less stressful surroundings.

The challenge of keeping bears from dying unnatural deaths and enabling them to live natural lives will never go away – not with millions of tourists flocking to Banff National Park each year. But those very visitors themselves can become a powerful constituency for bears and wild places.

As long as national park managers continue to control development, educate park visitors, promote mutual respect between bears and humans and still make difficult, sometimes unpopular decisions about restricting access to the most important bear habitats, tourism in the national parks is likely to serve as a force for the conservation of bears rather than as a threat to their future.

Jasper and Yoho National Parks in Canada, and Yellowstone and Yosemite in the US, share many of Banff's development challenges, including hotels and development right in the middle of prime bear habitat. Other national parks, like Rocky Mountain, Glacier and Kootenay, have mostly avoided the internal development conflicts that plague the older parks, but gateway communities just outside the parks, like Estes Park, West Glacier and Radium Hot Springs, sometimes put bears into conflict with humans.

Land speculators see national parks as prime locations for development. Since the parks themselves are protected – with the exception of some of Canada's mountain parks, where commercial interests like ski hills managed to get a toehold before the door slammed shut – most real estate development pressure is on ranches and farmland along the park boundaries. But bears don't recognize boundaries; they live in bear habitat wherever it may be found. Resort development doesn't need to be inside a park to put bear populations at risk.

Developers seeking approval for new ski hills, golf courses or condominiums near national parks rarely worry that their profits come at the expense of bears, even while they earnestly describe their investment schemes as environmentally friendly in order to win development approvals and attract customers. From ranchettes in Colorado's Sawatch and Elk Mountains, to resort subdivisions in Paradise Valley outside of Yellowstone, to four-season resorts in the Castle River valley north of Waterton Lakes National Park – wherever local governments fail to protect agricultural land adjacent to national parks from speculation – tourism and recreational second-home development continue to expropriate the wild places bears need for survival.

Andy Russell.

Andy Russell's Grizzly Country

Andy Russell was four years old in 1919 when his family moved to the spectacular aspen parkland country that sprawls along the foot of the Rocky Mountains, south of Pincher Creek.

He grew up exploring the canyons and headwaters of the Rocky Mountain front, hunting big game, fishing and running into the occasional bear. Those explorations served him well when, in 1936, he went to work for legendary outfitter Bert Riggall.

In 1937 Andy married Bert Riggall's oldest daughter, Kay, and a few years later they took over her father's outfitting business. For several years Kay and Andy continued to guide hunters, fishermen and adventurers into the wilderness of the upper Oldman, Castle and Flathead Rivers.

But the Alberta and BC governments wanted to develop oil, coal and timber resources, not protect wilderness. The governments pushed new roads into once-quiet valleys until Andy could no longer offer clients the solitude, untrammelled countryside and abundant wildlife his father-in-law had taken for granted. Even Waterton Lakes National Park, though spared industrial development, was becoming too tame and regulated as its popularity with tourists grew.

"I knew that outfitting was finished, at least the way I'd known it," he said. "At the time we were one of the top three outfits on the continent, but I'd seen what happened to some of these other guys who tried to hang on after it was too late, and I decided it was time to change careers." In 1960 Andy and Kay closed down the outfitting business Bert Riggall had started half a century earlier.

Andy instead became a wildlife cinematographer and conservation educator. He contracted for two short wildlife films, and then, with his oldest boys, Dick and Charlie, embarked on a major project to film grizzlies in the shrinking wildernesses of Waterton Lakes National Park, BC's Flathead valley and remote northern Alaska.

The resulting movie, *Grizzly Country*, is a remarkable chronicle of an animal that depended, like Andy himself, on an undervalued and fast-vanishing heritage: wilderness. The Russells made the entire film without even the protection of a rifle, working at close range with animals then considered the deadliest predators in North America. Learning as they went, about the tolerant side of the great bears, Andy and his sons soon began to challenge conventional wisdom that all bears are dangerous.

Andy toured North America with the film for eleven years, showing unprecedented images to audiences in Boston, New York, Toronto and dozens of other cities.

Grizzly country.

"That was a tough way to make a living – living out of a suitcase, having to deal with different strangers all the time." But everywhere he went, his movie played to packed houses, often to standing-room-only crowds. Andy's down-to-earth narration, a skill honed around countless flickering campfires, held them spellbound. His footage showed real grizzly bears, not the savage killers of myth.

Movies cost a lot to produce, so Andy decided to write a book to recover his costs. He flew to New York and had lunch with the editor-in-chief of the publishing house Alfred A. Knopf.

"I showed him a selection of one hundred or so wild-life photographs I'd brought out with me," said Andy. "There were pictures there of the head and shoulders of a grizzly, all kinds of wildlife photos. He just looked at them for a while, and then he said, 'Andy, how the hell did you manage to get pictures like this?' I said, 'That's what I'm here for: I want to write you a book that will tell exactly how I got those pictures.'"

Grizzly Country, the book, was published in 1967 and became an instant bestseller. Over one hundred thousand copies have sold so far around the world. *Grizzly Country's* anecdotal style and in-depth, sympathetic portrayal of grizzlies and the threats to their wilderness habitat played a pivotal role in building public awareness of the value and vulnerability of bears and other wildlife.

Andy Russell died in June 2005, at the age of eighty-nine – a lifelong champion of both grizzly bears and the wilderness where they thrive best.

Inspired by Andy's legacy, conservation groups are working now to restore the whole of his grizzly country. Hunting organizations, regional environmental groups and national foundations have joined together into the Yellowstone to Yukon Conservation Initiative (Y2Y). Their goal: to restore the ecological health and connectivity of the entire Rocky Mountain chain so that bears and wilderness will survive, not just in old books and films, but in reality.

It's an ambitious plan. Today's mountain landscape is fragmented by roads, clear-cuts, mines and resorts – the "multiple abuse" Andy railed against for half a century. But early successes – like the Nature Conservancy of Canada's Waterton Park Front project and the BC government's decision, in 2011, to permanently ban mining in the North Fork Flathead River drainage – point the way.

At the very heart of the Y2Y region, the Castle-Crown Wilderness Coalition has worked for years to persuade the Alberta government to honour its 1992 promise to protect the spectacular grizzly country into which Andy and Kay once led their clients. The coalition's proposal for a new wilderness park in his memory faces resistance by a small but politically influential group of loggers, off-road vehicle enthusiasts and ranchers.

Should the proposed Andy Russell–I'tai sah kòp Park become a reality, it would be a fitting memorial for one of Canada's great conservationists.

Maureen Enns's Grizzly Kingdom

Artist Maureen Enns lives today in an entirely different world than the one she thought she knew two decades ago. Her art, which for fifteen years focused on the grizzly bears of western Canada and Russia's Kamchatka Peninsula, reflects the profound changes in her consciousness.

In the early 1990s, after finishing a major art project on African elephants, Maureen turned her attention to home ground. "I wanted to say something about the Canadian wilderness. I've lived in the eastern slopes of the Rocky Mountains for about eighteen years and I thought, well, it's under fire just like everywhere else in the world. I thought of the grizzly as monarch of the mountains, the animal that represented the wildest of the wild country."

Maureen spent almost three years in the Banff National Park backcountry with park warden Rick Kunelius. Soon she was encountering an animal she had always thought of as fiercely dangerous, wild and aloof. But the behaviour of these bears didn't align with her preconceived notions.

"I sort of grew up with certain expectations about

grizzlies: if they're in the area, they're going to cause trouble; if your horse gets near one, it'll probably buck you off; and if you get between a mother and her cubs or a bear and its kill, it'll charge instantly...

"Well, once during the first year, I rode over this knoll and surprised some little grizzly cubs about thirty feet away. I couldn't see their mother. Then I spotted her, and she was just covered with blood! She'd just killed an elk ... But my horse didn't seem all that upset.

"The mother just sort of looked at us and moseyed around. Her cubs scampered over to her, and she just wandered away and nothing happened."

As Maureen had more unexpectedly peaceful encounters with the great bears, her art changed. At first, reds and blacks predominated and the bears were out-lined and isolated on the canvas, reflecting the artist's

Maureen Enns and her painting Queen of the Rockies.

Lilly's Cubs on Wonder Pass, *by Maureen Enns.*

own fears and isolation. Gradually the colours softened and bears began to emerge into their own landscapes.

By the end of her first project, Maureen realized she had only begun to know bears for what they really were.

Maureen's questions brought her into contact with Charlie Russell, a rancher-biologist on his own quest for a better understanding of the animals. Their common passion for bears led to another, more ambitious project: several summers in the windswept wilderness of Russia's Kamchatka Peninsula.

Kamchatka has the highest density of brown bears in the world. Here Maureen and Charlie lived for months on end with only bears for company. Each year they rescued orphaned bear cubs from captivity and spent the summer teaching them to live in the wild.

While Charlie tested his theory that bears and humans can interact without fear or conflict, Maureen spent many days sitting in bear beds – well-worn traditional bedding areas used by generations of brown bears – seeking her own understanding of a bear's sense of its surroundings. Increasingly her canvases became intricately detailed with colours of lichen, blueberry and moss. The bears became individual beings whose facial expressions and body language reflected their interactions with one another and the world around them – as well as Maureen's increasingly profound understanding of the true nature of bears.

The Kamchatka years ended in tragedy. Poachers killed all the bears in the area, including all the rescued cubs. "Coming out of the Russia project I was quite bitter ... I just thought I'd never again get involved with animals that are misunderstood and that eventually probably would all get killed for some reason or other."

But upon her return to the Alberta Rockies, Maureen found herself among bears again. When Rick Kunelius invited her to join him in 2007 at Mount Assiniboine Lodge in the BC Rockies to train lodge staff and their guests on how to coexist safely with the many grizzlies that occupied the area, Maureen felt compelled to go. In Kamchatka she had learned to read how bears communicated with their posture, and had practised using similar body language along with her voice to defuse tense situations. At Mount Assiniboine she taught these skills to others, including some Olympic athletes who were using the mountain trails for training runs.

"I showed them what young bears will do with an older bear, rotate their body and chew on something just to pretend they don't care at all, and then that dissipates the confrontation. And I showed them how you talk at the same time and the bears sort of get lulled into being relaxed. And to always get out your bear spray, while this is going on, just in case.

"But I said, for sure you're going to have a bear chase you down the trail someday, because these young bears either get excited when they hear the running, or they see something moving and they want to go after it. What you've got to do is stop immediately and step off the trail and do the body language thing and chat to them.

"And it was a week later that one girl was running down the trail, and this young bear gallops down the trail after her, right hot on her heels. And she just stepped off the trail and she told us, 'I did exactly everything that you said, and it just sat down and started to chew on some plants.' And then she walked back."

Among the Mount Assiniboine bears was a mother with three cubs. Maureen and Rick became particularly fond of the gentle mother bear, whom they named Lily. She was completely at ease around the hundreds of people who visited the area that summer, thanks in part to the lodge owners and staff who encouraged visitors to be calm around the bears and to enjoy them from a distance.

After the trauma of losing all the Kamchatka bears, Maureen had been sure she would never draw or paint a bear again. But her time with Lily and her family helped her come to a different understanding.

"I wasn't going to do bears ever again, but it was almost like I had to... I thought about the bears we loved so much that we raised. And I thought, well, you've got to honour what those bears taught you."

TOURISM FOR BEARS

In spite of tourism's generally poor track record, a growing trend away from conventional facility-based tourism to environmentally responsible ecotourism offers the intriguing possibility that tourism may become a force for the conservation, rather than destruction, of North America's bears.

Ecotourism is based on the idea that healthy wildlife populations and unspoiled natural habitats – not resorts and other man-made attractions – are the most valuable capital assets for western Canada's tourism industry. Ecotourism operators offer high-quality, nature-based experiences with highly skilled guides, rather than luxury accommodations, spas and convention facilities in the heart of what was once wild nature. Rather than seeing wilderness protection as an obstacle to tourism, these business people see it as critical to their industry's success.

Commercial wildlife-viewing tour operators and whitewater rafting companies played a major role in the twentieth century in building public demand for protected wilderness areas in BC. The provincial government designated the immense Tatshenshini River watershed a wilderness reserve and cancelled a planned copper mine after commercial rafting operators took journalists, politicians and other influential people for wilderness excursions down the river. Similarly, it was ecotourism operators who helped argue, successfully, that the Khutzeymateen watershed near Prince Rupert was worth more to the province of BC as a protected bear sanctuary than as just another logged-out valley.

In the mid-1980s, Beth Russell-Towe conceived one of the earliest and most visionary efforts to make tourism a force for bear conservation. A business operator in Waterton Lakes National Park, Beth was also concerned about the rate of habitat fragmentation around the great national parks in the US and Canadian Rockies. She knew that if parks become completely isolated, their bear populations become increasingly vulnerable to extinction. Without their great bears, the parks would lose not just their ecological wholeness, but their souls.

Beth conceived of a tourism marketing concept now known internationally as "Trail of the Great Bear." The trail is actually a network of scenic travel routes that connect Yellowstone National Park – the first national park in the US and home of the southernmost surviving population of North American grizzlies – with Banff (the first in Canada) and Jasper National Parks by way of Waterton–Glacier, the world's first international peace park. By linking the entire tourism corridor to grizzly bear habitat, Beth and others in the tourism industry hope to give other business people a stake in promoting conservation of bear habitat in the entire region, not just the parks. At the same time, tourists from around the world now find more and better opportunities to learn about grizzly bears and their habitat as they travel the Trail of the Great Bear through some of the most spectacular bear country in the Rocky Mountains.

The Waterton Front

Tourists travel to the spectacular 505-square-kilometre Waterton Lakes National Park hoping to see its bears, both black and grizzly. En route, they traverse a ranching landscape where, conventional wisdom might suggest, bears are not welcome.

But those ranches are at least as important to the survival of Waterton's bear population as the national park itself.

Waterton used to include a lot more of the foothill forests, as well as the headwaters of the Castle River and other streams north of its current boundaries. But when Canada's federal government gave the Province of Alberta control over land and resources, it also shrank the park boundaries to exclude any land that had agricultural or forestry value.

Today's small national park still has good bear habitat – just not as much as it needs. The most productive bear country lies outside the park boundary, where bears have to share the lush aspen thickets, spring-fed wetlands and green stream valleys with domestic cattle on neighbouring ranches. Fortunately, this landscape is close to protected bear populations in Montana and the bear-rich Flathead valley of BC. Besides, most area ranchers figured out long ago how to coexist with bears, and consequently the area has among the highest densities in the province of each species of bears.

This happy state of affairs came under threat in the 1990s, when real estate developers, attracted by the scenery and recreational amenities in the national park, began to knock on ranch house doors, looking for willing sellers. The land speculators hoped to subdivide and develop ranchland for recreational properties and second homes.

Ironically it was not ranching that had become a threat to the area's bears, but the national park itself. A location next to a national park is a gold mine for a

The Waterton Front.

developer. The land prices adjacent to the park – higher than elsewhere in western Alberta – soon tempted some ranchers to sell and created more tax pressure for the rest.

Waterton's neighbours had previously fought off similar development threats, but this time was different. Some area ranchers were in financial difficulty or growing too old to keep up with the hard work. Municipal authorities wanted new tax revenues. A booming provincial economy meant that developers had access to capital and buyers.

A major cottage development proposal against the park boundary brought matters to a head in 1997. Just as municipal approval seemed imminent, the Nature Conservancy of Canada (NCC) bought the property from the developer. Most of the locals had never heard of the NCC before. Soon, everyone had.

Over the ensuing decade, visionary Canadian philanthropists such as John and Barbara Poole and the W. Garfield Weston Foundation helped the NCC protect more than one hundred square kilometres of ranching landscape from development forever. The NCC's Waterton Park Front project ultimately raised more than $50-million to purchase conservation easements, retire development rights and, where necessary, buy land outright and then lease it back to ranchers. One of the largest private land conservation efforts in Canada's history, it secured the future for both bears and ranchers.

Blaine Marr's family ranch in Oil Basin is a secluded swath of exceptionally well cared for native grassland, aspen forest and wetlands where bears and other wildlife thrive. After working with the NCC to place conservation easements on his property, Blaine explained his rationale in a newspaper interview: "Our land is a unique spot. We've learned to manage it over the last three generations, and I wanted to see it stay the way it is."

For well more than a century, ranching ensured that bear habitat adjacent to Waterton Lakes National Park remained intact and healthy. Thanks to the NCC, this green and healthy landscape that sprawls along the edge of the Rocky Mountains will continue to sustain both ranching families and bear families well into the future.

www.natureconservancy.ca

3
REAL BEARS

BEARS IN PREHISTORY

The earliest bears appear in the fossil record from the Miocene geological epoch, about twenty million years ago. Bears have been around a lot longer than humans. They appear to have descended from Miacids, a long-extinct line of little tree-climbing creatures that also gave rise to the modern dog and seal families. An early creation myth of the Tahltan people of BC's Stikine Plateau, coincidentally, seems to reflect the common evolutionary origin of seals and bears. According to this myth, the first people were threatened by an immense flood; those who fled up into the forest became bears, while those who ended up in the water became seals.

In any case, the earliest bear-like animals evolved along three different evolutionary lines. Two died out long ago, and the third, which first appeared about three million years ago, eventually gave rise to all eight modern bear species.

The earliest ancestors of grizzly, black and cave bears all originated around 2.5 million years ago in Asia. The cave bear – almost twice the size of our modern grizzly – was extinct by the time the ancestors of North American black bears ventured east, more than a

Coastal grizzlies fish for salmon.

million years ago, across the low-lying plains that once joined Siberia to Alaska.

Compared to the black bear, grizzlies (the same species as Europe's brown bears) were latecomers. They arrived in Alaska toward the end of the last Ice Age and only spread south across North America after the continental ice sheets had melted back, some twelve to fifteen thousand years ago. Some biologists believe grizzly bears were still expanding their range eastward toward the Atlantic when they encountered Europeans spreading west with their guns and strychnine.

That marked the end of range expansion for the grizzly and the beginning of a retreat that for the most part continues today.

WHAT ARE BEARS?

Bears belong to the order *Carnivora*, along with dogs, cats, weasels and raccoons. All carnivores have sharp, elongated canine teeth for puncturing and tearing flesh, and specially designed molars for slicing and shredding. They also have highly refined senses and learning abilities, important attributes for animals that must hunt for their food.

But black bears and grizzlies – western North America's two modern bear species – only occasionally dine on meat, unlike most other carnivores. They are opportunistic omnivores, eating vegetable matter most of the time but taking advantage, when they can, of temporary abundances of fish, insects or meat. Bears have special adaptations for this uncarnivorous diet – an elongated gut that enables them to extract more food value from vegetable matter than other carnivores (though still far less than deer, elk and other ruminants) and front molars adapted for crushing rather than slicing.

The flat-footed gait of bears is another characteristic that sets them apart from other carnivores. Bears lay down their entire sole and all five toes with each step. The elongated soles of their hind feet leave tracks similar to those of a human. Their characteristic gait is a shuffling four-legged walk, but bears can walk on their hind legs for a short distance. A bear in a hurry can run much faster than a human – grizzlies have been clocked at forty-five kilometres per hour over short distances.

Bears of the world

Only eight species of bear exist in the world, and all but the black bear are listed by the International Union for Conservation of Nature as being at risk of extinction. Black, grizzly and polar bears are found in North America. The remaining five species are:

Giant panda: the most endangered of all bears – it is possible that fewer than five hundred pandas still survive in the wild. Pandas are uniquely different from other bear species in many ways. Their eyes have slit-like vertical pupils similar to those of foxes and cats – this probably accounts for the panda's Chinese name, which translates to "giant cat-bear." Pandas depend on bamboo forests for both shelter and food, but growing human populations in China are replacing bamboo with agricultural fields. The panda is the symbol of the World Wildlife Fund.

Asiatic black bear: similar in many ways to our American black bear, this species appears to have evolved from a common ancestor. It ranges from Pakistan and Afghanistan east to the Pacific Ocean. Many populations have been decimated in recent years due to demand for their gallbladders in Chinese and Korean markets. Asian black bears are also frequently killed as agricultural pests because of their habit of stripping bark from trees and eating the underlying sapwood.

Sloth bear: living in the forests of southern Asia, the sloth bear derives its name in part from the females' habit of carrying their cubs on their backs. Fewer than ten thousand survive in the wild, due to the ongoing loss of their forest habitats to clear-cutting by multinational forest companies. Sloth bears eat ants, termites and honey in addition to vegetation and carrion.

Sun bear: barely half the size of our black bear, the sun bear is the smallest species in the world. Most look disarmingly like black bear cubs, but sun bears are known to attack humans on occasion. Dependent on lowland tropical forests in southeastern Asia, sun bears face multiple threats. Deforestation is destroying their habitat in many areas, the gallbladder trade has led to increasing hunting pressure, and coconut plantation owners shoot the little bears to protect their trees. Biologists are concerned that the sun bear may become extinct before scientists have even documented basic biological information about it.

Spectacled bear: the only species in South America, the spectacled bear appears to have evolved from a giant, long-legged bear that once ranged throughout the western hemisphere. Fewer than two thousand survive in the wild, because growing populations of slash-and-burn farmers, displaced from fertile lowlands by large companies that grow coffee, bananas and other luxury crops for export, are gradually destroying the cloud forest habitat upon which these bears depend.

How big is a bear?

	Weight	Length
Polar bear	300–550 kg (660–1200 lb)	1.5–3 m (6–11 ft)
Grizzly	130–400 kg (280–900 lb)	1.8–2.5 m (5.5–7.5 ft)
Black bear	90–150 kg (200–325 lb)	1.2–1.9 m (3.7–6.0 ft)

Black bear or grizzly?

It isn't always easy to tell bears apart. Many people, seeing a brown-coloured bear, assume they have spotted a grizzly, but colour is really of little help in distinguishing the two species. The name "grizzly" comes from the grizzled appearance of many grizzlies, caused by pale guard hairs protruding from a darker coat – but not all grizzlies are grizzled. Grizzly bears can range in colour from whitish to nearly black. Although grizzlies in the Rocky Mountains are often silver-tipped, coastal ones tend to be brown. Black bears, in turn, can be black, brown, slate-blue, honey-coloured or even white.

Size isn't reliable either, since large black bears can be twice the size of small grizzlies. Habitat is a useful clue – grizzlies are more of an open-country species – but, again, both species overlap extensively.

So how do you know what you're looking at? The important distinguishing features are in the shape and proportion of the bear's body:

Grizzly	
	• smaller-looking, rounded ears • snout protrudes from "dish-shaped" face • ruff of coarse hair beneath chin • usually have a pronounced hump at shoulders; adults generally seem taller at shoulders than at rump • long, often pale-coloured claws
Black bear	
	• larger, more elongated ears • snout and forehead tend to run together in a straight line • smooth throat • little or no hump; adults usually appear taller at rump than at shoulders • claws dark, short, rarely noticeable

HIBERNATION

Bears sleep through the winter, unlike wolves, foxes and cougars, which continue to hunt and travel about. Black bears often dig out a den under the roots of a tree or, in the temperate rainforests of BC and the Pacific Northwest, curl up in the hollow interior of an old cedar tree. Grizzlies that range the mountainous interior of North America usually excavate a den at high elevations where heavy layers of winter snow will insulate them. Those that live in coastal rainforests sometimes use hollow trees.

Many hibernators, like ground squirrels, become icy cold, their body temperatures dropping close to freezing. From time to time the little animals may waken briefly to eat, urinate, or perform other bodily functions. The rest of the time, they are so deeply unconscious that nothing can stir their slumbers.

A bear does not interrupt its hibernation to eat or urinate, so in some ways its winter sleep is more profound than that of a hibernating rodent. Bears still lose body moisture through breathing and evaporation, but they replace the lost moisture by burning stored fat. In the absence of urination, this would poison the bear eventually – a condition known as uremia – if weren't for a unique aspect of bear metabolism that lets them convert urea and other toxic by-products into protein.

In other ways, though, a bear's hibernation is less pronounced than a rodent's. A bear's body temperature drops only seven or eight degrees Celsius below normal, and body functions like heartbeat and breathing slow down only to somewhat less than half of normal. Bears remain warm and can be easily wakened. Since that requires continuing metabolism, their bodies need a lot of stored-up energy for fuel. Black and grizzly bears, burning stored fat to stay alive, may lose more than a quarter of their total body weight between the time they go to bed in the fall and breakfast time several months later.

Bear fat is exceptionally rich in energy, yielding more than 7,500 calories per kilogram; a fat adult male grizzly, then, can curl up for his winter nap with as much as 2.5 million calories of energy stored in rolls beneath his grizzled hide. He'll need it; a hibernating bear can burn up to four thousand calories of energy per day just to keep from freezing. A female bear with less than 20 per cent body fat when she goes into her den will not give birth to cubs; instead, her body reabsorbs the embryos so that she can use her limited energy to stay alive.

HUNGER

There are few fat vegetarians at the salad bar. That, for a bear, is the whole problem. Their need to accumulate a copious supply of fat before winter forces bears to concentrate intently on the life-and-death challenge of finding energy-rich food during the rest of the year.

That bear ambling from one berry bush to another beside the road may look, to watching tourists, like it is enjoying a lazy day in the woods. In reality, it is involved in the deadly serious task of building fat for next winter. It can't afford time off or distractions. Displacing a bear from a good feeding area forces it to waste energy searching for another.

Although meat tops the list of high-quality food, bears are poorly designed for chasing down other animals. Most bears have to settle for taking over the carcasses of animals killed by other predators, disease or accidents. Some bears, however, become very effective

Black bear munching dandelions.

predators of newborn elk, moose, deer or caribou. Others are fortunate enough to live in areas where salmon, suckers or other fish spawn in large numbers for part of each year.

Bears spend most of their time feeding on vegetation, insects or other food sources that are more reliable, if less energy-rich, than meat. Most bears continue to lose weight through early spring because of the scarcity of these sources of food early in the year, but they make up for the loss in summer, when they may gain more than a kilogram a day.

Bears eat a lot to compensate for the fact that vegetable matter and other consistently available food sources don't yield a lot of food energy. Their digestive systems are effective at extracting the starches, proteins and other easily digested components of these foods, and the remainder is excreted undigested. Bear scat is consequently a useful clue to a bear's diet, since ants, green plants and berries are usually still recognizable in the remains.

Big eaters

A bear can consume up to twenty thousand calories of food energy a day, according to studies of captive animals. That's the equivalent of 130 baked potatoes with sour cream, or 30 hamburgers.

Where do they get that much food energy? Some Yukon researchers painstakingly examined a collection of wild grizzly droppings to find part of the answer. They found that a grizzly may eat as many as one hundred thousand buffalo berries each day at the peak of berry season.

What do bears eat?

	Meat	Fish	Vegetation	Insects
Polar bear	95%	5%	0%	0%
Grizzly	10%	5%*	80%	5%
Black bear	15%	0%*	75%	10%
*considerably more in coastal drainages where salmon and other fish congregate to spawn.				

The best foods for bears vary depending on the habitats available in any given area, and also on the season. A plant that is highly nutritious in spring may be low in value later in the summer. Berries are only available in certain habitats late in the summer, but dry or cool summers can result in berry crop failures, forcing bears to wander widely in search of alternative foods.

Bears, then, tend to migrate across large home ranges, using different parts of the landscape at different times, depending on where the best source of food is at any given season. This is crucial, because a bear that goes to bed in poor condition is very unlikely to be alive come the spring.

JUNK FOOD

When a bear catches wind of human garbage, barbecues, poorly stored food or anything that promises sustenance, it is likely to find the temptation irresistible. Bears can't afford to turn their backs on something their nose tells them will yield a lot of body fat for little effort.

Most national parks, from their very beginnings, had open garbage dumps and small garbage cans – infamously known as "bear feeders" – in all their high-use areas. Inevitably, bears discovered these food sources. Their compulsive need for high-energy food soon overpowered any aversion they might have had to being near people. Park rangers and wardens grew to dread each year's cycle that saw some bears becoming more and more comfortable around humans, then becoming aggressive, and finally having to be killed to protect park visitors.

Some park officials opted for extreme measures: biologist Wayne McCrory says that in the early 1970s, wardens in BC's Glacier National Park had orders to

A black bear rummages through garbage at an open dump site.

shoot grizzly bears on sight. After Parks Canada electrified the fence at the Jasper National Park landfill in the late 1970s, I saw a notice in the warden office instructing wardens to kill black bears on sight in and around the townsite. And they did: thirty-four black bears died at the hands of park staff that year.

After the 1968 closure of Yellowstone National Park garbage dumps, bears that had become accustomed to easy pickings moved into developed areas. The result: a dramatic increase in both reported and unreported shootings of problem bears. Throughout the West, some heavily used campgrounds acted like ecological vacuum cleaners, attracting bears from the surrounding landscape. Between 1950 and 1980, wardens in Banff and Jasper National Parks reported killing 523 black bears and relocating another 547. The actual death toll was much higher – park authorities often didn't bother to document dead bears.

The 1970s and 1980s brought new awareness and new technology to western national parks. Killing bears to solve garbage and food storage problems – never popular with most rangers and wardens – had become less acceptable to the public. Following the controversial closure of Yellowstone's garbage dumps, park managers in Banff, Jasper and other national parks followed suit. Canadian national parks went a step further, replacing traditional garbage cans with bear-proof dumpsters. Many parks ultimately joined forces with neighbouring communities to build electric-fenced regional landfills that completely exclude bears.

Park interpretive programs and strict enforcement of rules also reduced the supply of poorly stored food for scavenging bears in campgrounds. By the late 1980s, very few tourists were stupid or stubborn enough to offer handouts to bears. Few bears now die in national parks because of food or garbage problems – a remarkable conservation success story.

Elsewhere in bear country, however, some towns and settlements continue to tempt bears to death. Recreational cabins in Montana's North Fork Flathead valley, for example, attract grizzly bears to dog food, stored oats and garbage so often that the state employs bear experts solely to save bears from temptation. Farther north, a municipal landfill near Sparwood, BC, resulted in the loss of sixty bears – a third of which were grizzlies – in 1995 alone.

From 1986 to 1995, Wayne McCrory counted 106 grizzlies killed, or trapped and relocated, from the vicinity of the Revelstoke, BC, dump. "Many of those," he says, "were from the nearby national parks."

Mike Reid is a wildlife manager in Pagosa Springs, Colorado. Describing his frustration with rural residents whose sloppiness too often dooms bears to untimely ends, he says, "Most people seem to know that they shouldn't let bears get food from them, but then they go ahead and put their trash out two days early. While we're busy informing the public through newspaper articles and radio programs, the public is busy educating the bears about human food. So far, it seems the bears are the quick learners."

Only you can prevent bear deaths
"Every person who contributes to habituating bears by feeding them, by leaving garbage at campsites or along

roads, by not handling food properly, by not taking care of fruit trees, pet foods, barbecues or other attractants around the home or farm, is responsible for the loss of bears."

Why not just move the bears?

Midnight. A few campfires still flicker here and there, but the campground is still and quiet. The night is growing cold; cicadas have ceased their trilling and dew is beginning to condense on the tents and trailers.

Soft footfalls crunch on gravel. A black shape, darker than the forest shadows, stops at the edge of the campground, sniffing. Then it turns and steps soundlessly

Two bears investigate a culvert trap.

into a gap in the trees where a large culvert on wheels is parked behind a ribbon of yellow tape. The ripe, rich smell of dead beaver emanates from the dark interior.

The bear hoists himself into the culvert and grabs the bait at the far end. The door clangs shut, jarring the midnight stillness.

Another campground bear is going for a ride.

To deal with bears that have become food-addicted thanks to the sloppiness of campers, a tool in general use by park rangers and wildlife officials is the culvert trap. More rarely, they use heavy-duty cable snares designed to hold the bear's paw but not cut off blood circulation. The advantage of snares is that they work on animals too shy to enter a culvert trap or in too remote a location for the culvert trap to be moved into place. The disadvantage is that bears often hurt themselves struggling against the snare. Some suffer lasting injuries or even die later.

Once officers have snared a bear, they use a specially designed gun to fire a tranquilizer dart and then haul the unconscious animal away. Often, if it's a black bear, they end up killing it. In national parks, however, and with most grizzlies – depending on the history of the bear – the officers may try to save its life by releasing it somewhere far from where they caught it.

The problem with trapping and relocating bears, however, is that too often it doesn't work. There are no longer places where a bear that has learned to associate humans with food can be released without a high likelihood that it will find more humans and get back into trouble again.

Even if a bear can be dropped off in a suitably remote area, there is no way to make it stay there. One grizzly bear released near Manning, Alberta, in 1995 was subsequently shot by a hunter in the Yukon's St. Elias Mountains. Bears have wandered more than six hundred kilometres from release sites, often returning home, where they again get into trouble.

Relocating spoiled bears can work under some circumstances. Biologists in Glacier National Park monitored twenty-two different grizzly bears trapped and moved because of conflict with humans. Sixteen of those relocations were considered successful: the bear did not return or get into trouble again. All the bears that were moved more than 120 kilometres from the point of capture remained out of trouble, while most of those moved shorter distances became repeat offenders. Relocating females, which tend to wander over much smaller areas, was more successful than moving males.

One reason bears often don't stay where they're put: a bear finding itself in unfamiliar terrain may face conflict with the bears that already live there. If it stays, it stands a good chance of being killed. If it leaves, it also stands a good chance of being killed. Moving a bear, in other words, creates the illusion that the problem has been solved without the death of the bear when, too often, the bear simply dies later.

Wayne McCrory feels that relocating bears could be more successful if wildlife officers would put in the extra time and effort to subject the bear to electric shocks, pepper spray or other form of negative conditioning, to teach it that contact with humans can be painful. "It's mean," he acknowledges, "but it would save more bears' lives."

Charlie Russell disagrees. "I think it's terrible, because of what it's telling the bear. It's a deliberate way of saying that people are bad news. That works with some bears just as long as they stay away, but what about the surprise situation, and what about the bear that just lives on and on, never liking people, because its only experience is negative and then finally it just has enough? I don't think that happens very often, because bears seem to be very tolerant and they usually will get out of the way."

Most bear managers agree that nothing works so well as simply protecting bears from the temptation of poorly managed garbage or livestock. "If we have to relocate or destroy an animal," says Waterton Lakes National Park wildlife/human conflict specialist Rob Watt, "then we've failed. The system has failed."

A grizzly stands up to gain a better view of its surroundings.

Bear myths

Bears are dangerous and unpredictable predators.
Most encounters between humans and bears end peacefully. Like us, bears prefer to avoid conflict. They are capable of being dangerous, but unless surprised or frightened, they almost always choose not to.

Bears react to humans much like they do other bears; while they may act aggressive, they try to avoid actual contact. Only very rarely do they actually view us as prey. Bears, in fact, aren't properly considered predators. They are omnivores that spend most of their time foraging for plant, insect and other food, rather than actively hunting live prey.

Bears left in peace and treated with respect are predictable and rarely dangerous; we humans, on the other hand, can be far more unpredictable. That is often the real source of danger.

When a bear stands on its hind legs, it's about to charge.
When a bear stands on its hind legs, it's simply trying to see or smell something it is unsure about. A bear that is about to charge lays its ears back and lowers its body closer to the ground, fixing its eyes on the object of its aggression.

You should be okay if you don't get between a mother and her cubs.
It can be dangerous to find yourself between a mother bear and her cubs. But with grizzlies in particular, you risk your life by being anywhere around the cubs. What makes a situation dangerous is not where you are

standing: it's whether the mother perceives a threat to her young. Her job is to keep them safe. If she perceives one of us as a threat to her cubs, she may attack.

Male bears will adopt orphaned cubs.
James Oliver Curwood's 1916 novel *The Grizzly King* originated this idea, which was later popularized in the movie *The Bear*. In the real world, some adult male bears hunt and kill cubs. That's one reason female bears can be so aggressive about defending their young.

Bears can't run downhill.
This myth is probably based on the fact that bears appear to be lower at the front than at the back. It's dead wrong. Bears can run more than fifty kilometres (thirty miles) per hour. Humans can't run even half that speed.

There are too many bears.
This occasional complaint usually comes from people who leave garbage, unpicked fruit trees, animal carcasses or other temptation out where they will attract bears. Chronic problems with bears generally indicate human sloppiness with potential food sources, not a sudden overpopulation of bears. Bears will travel a long distance to investigate a promising scent.

Bears regulate their own numbers by avoiding one another. As bear numbers increase, so too does the potential for older bears to kill younger ones or force them to leave the area. Food supplies, and the amount of energy bears have to use in order to find food, further restrict the number of bears an area will support.

Temporary concentrations of bears in nature are usually the result of temporary abundance of foods like salmon, berries or carrion that draw bears from a much larger surrounding area.

Bears that lose their fear of people are dangerous.
Not necessarily. Bears aren't preconditioned to fear humans; fear is something they learn through experience when they are harassed or mistreated.

Some bears actually choose to be around people, perhaps because other bears avoid us. Female grizzlies in Alberta's Kananaskis Valley, for instance, keep their cubs in productive feeding habitats close to the highway, while larger male bears tend to avoid the road. Bears that treat humans as part of the scenery are often described as "neutral" bears – the least dangerous kind.

On the other hand, bears that associate humans with food are potentially very dangerous.

Charlie Russell's work has led him to conclude that bears that fear people may actually be more dangerous than those that don't. A bear suddenly confronted by a human has to make a split-second decision on how to react. A neutral bear that has no reason to fear humans is likely to relax or move out of the way. A fearful bear may flee ... but it might also attack in self-defence.

If a bear charges at you, climb a tree.
Climbing a tree won't help you escape a determined black bear. Black bears climb trees frequently to escape danger, hunt insects or feed on the buds and young leaves of poplar trees in spring.

Grizzlies are physically capable of climbing and will do so if sufficiently aroused, especially if the tree has strong branches. They normally don't, however, so climbing as far up a tree as possible may help you avoid an upset grizzly.

Humans and bears can't coexist without conflict.
In fact, we coexist well with bears in many areas, as anyone who lives in Canmore, West Glacier or Fernie can attest. Charlie Russell describes three large brown bears that walked every day through a fishing village in Russia's Kamchatka Peninsula to hunt salmon below the villagers' fishing weir. Even the village dogs ignored the bears, although they barked aggressively at strange bears when they appeared. The bears too were discreet and respectful in their contacts with humans. Similar interactions play out along popular salmon rivers in coastal Alaska each year.

Many aboriginal tribes inhabiting Canada's Pacific coastal drainages, living with bears day to day, have developed a strong affinity for the animals. In western North America most conflict between bears and humans results from poor waste management or lack of informed respect for bears, not from any intrinsic incompatibility between people and bears.

REPRODUCTION

Bears are among the least productive large mammals to roam the wilds of Canada. Since bears live long lives – some have been found to live more than twenty-five years in the wild – and have few enemies, they have little need for a high birth rate.

In theory, a male and female black bear born this year, if they bred as soon as they were sexually mature

Black bear cubs at play.

and as often thereafter as possible, and if their offspring did the same, could have grown to a population of fifteen bears after ten years – assuming none died. Grizzly bears are even less productive. A male and female born today could only increase to a total of eight over the same ten years.

By comparison, a pair of white-tailed deer born today could produce over 1,400 descendants in the same period of time! Little wonder that hunting seasons for deer are considerably more generous than those for bears.

The reason for the difference is that bears take up to five years to reach sexual maturity, and then only breed at two or three year intervals. Bears mature earlier, and

Bears produce fewer offspring than almost any other mammal.

produce larger litters, in areas where food is consistently abundant. Cub growth and survival rates are higher in good habitat too.

In western Canada, most bears mate in May or June. As females become receptive to breeding, males pick up their scent and quickly home in on them. The male has a lot of work cut out for him, since females may continually try to escape his attentions right up until the moment when they are finally ready. Other males, too, may try to cut in, leading to ferocious threat displays between the competitors and, occasionally, physical battles.

Once the female is ready, she may accept one to several males over the following week or so. Then the bears separate to pursue the vitally important business of gaining weight for the winter.

In contrast to the reproductive process for most other animals, the fertilized eggs do not attach to the female bear's uterine wall until she goes into her winter den late in the fall. Even then, if she is in poor condition because of illness, injury or lack of food, the embryos may be reabsorbed into her body. Delayed implantation is a sort of insurance policy for both female and cubs, allowing her to put all her energy into fattening up through the summer and fall.

The tiny cubs – small enough to fit into one hand – are born in the winter den late in mid-winter as cold winds howl outside. Black bears are born naked and grizzlies with fur, but all bear cubs are blind at birth and remain that way for the first few weeks, during which time they grow rapidly. Bear cubs can be noisy, especially when they lose physical contact with their mothers. A cub that can't share its mother's body heat will die.

Bears breed slowly!

	Age at sexual maturity: Females	Age at sexual maturity: Males	Number of young per litter	Maximum years between litters*	Theoretical increase from 2 in 10 yrs
Polar bear	5–7	5–7	1–3	2	11
Grizzly	5–7	5–7	1–3	3	8
Black bear	4–5	5–6	1–4	2	15
White-tailed deer	2	2	1–3	1	14–24
* assuming the two were born in first year and all litters were equal parts males and females; that they bred at the earliest possible maturity and had the largest normal litter each time; and that there were no deaths.					

How big is a bear's home?

Bears don't occupy exclusive territories where other bears aren't allowed. Instead, each bear occupies a home range that overlaps with those of other bears. They avoid conflict simply by choosing to avoid each other most of the time.

The closest human analogy to a bear's home range might be the area that includes our home, where we work, the stores where we shop, and our favourite recreation places. Like bears, we tolerate the presence of other humans within our home range as long as they don't invade our personal space, compete with us too directly for things we want, threaten our offspring or belongings or come into our homes without an invitation.

A bear's home range can change in size from one year to the next or from one area to another, depending on how food and other habitat needs are distributed across the landscape. Mother bears with small cubs usually occupy very small home ranges that expand as their cubs grow. Bears need to cover a lot of ground in order to find the food they need from one season to the next; as a result, bears are considerably less abundant than most other large animals, even under the most ideal circumstances. Bears have smaller home ranges in areas like the BC coast that are rich in bear foods like salmon and berries, while those that live in less productive habitats like the Rocky Mountains or the far north necessarily range over much larger areas.

	square km	square mi.
Calgary	1,200	460
Banff National Park	6,640	2,560
Greater Vancouver	2,800	1,000
Waterton Lakes National Park	525	202

Home-range sizes:

		square km	square mi.
Grizzly	male	1,000–2,500	385–965
	female	200–500	80–200
Black bear	male	100–475	40–180
	female	20–300	8–115

HOW BEARS DIE

The biggest threat to bears is death at the hands of human beings, but other bears can sometimes be a hazard too. Some male bears actively hunt and kill young bears, especially where bear population densities are high. That's why female bears can be so aggressive in defence of their offspring. Young bears are particularly vulnerable during the first few weeks after they leave their mothers, when they are alone, naive and often exploring unfamiliar terrain.

When researchers killed most of the adult male black bears in a study area near Cold Lake, Alberta, the bear population actually doubled, apparently because more cubs and yearlings were able survive to adulthood.

Cub predation by males makes a sort of evolutionary sense. A female who has lost her cubs goes into heat soon after, increasing the odds that the male who killed them will get to breed her. The tendency of some males to be aggressive toward other bears also helps to keep population densities fairly low and bears well spaced around the landscape, which reduces pressure on food supplies.

Under natural conditions, bear populations survive

Coexistence is a challenge when bears and humans congregate to fish for salmon in the same place.

because their low reproductive rate is balanced by a low death rate. Although there may sometimes be a small surplus, it doesn't take a big increase in the death rate to change this balance and send a bear population into decline.

Food supplies can vary from year to year depending on the weather and other factors. When a cold growing season or a long drought results in a failure of the local berry crop, or some other factor temporarily cuts off an important food supply, weaker bears may succumb to starvation and others may wander far afield in search of alternative foods. Wandering bears may end up in farm country, near towns or along roads where they are likely to be killed by humans.

Where food supplies are particularly abundant – for example at a garbage dump, along a salmon spawning stream or in an area with many winter-killed animals – the antipathy of bears for one another breaks down and several may be seen feeding almost shoulder-to-shoulder. Normally, however, bears avoid each other because of the danger of an encounter turning ugly.

John and Frank Craighead studied grizzlies for almost two decades in Yellowstone National Park. They calculated that about 10 per cent of the area's grizzlies died each year because of hunting outside the park (legal at the time) and management kills by park rangers. The population managed to hold its own until officials abruptly closed down the park's garbage dumps in the late 1960s. Bears that had become dependent on the dumps wandered into campgrounds and towns in search of replacement food, became problems, and were killed in unprecedented numbers. As the death rate from management kills climbed above 20 per cent, the population began to drop alarmingly.

Fortunately the surviving bears learned to concentrate on natural foods, and grizzly hunting ended when Yellowstone's bears were designated an endangered species in the mid-1970s. Since then, grizzly numbers have recovered to the point where they are more abundant in the Yellowstone ecosystem than at any time in recorded history. From fewer than two hundred in the late 1960s, the estimated population has grown to more than six hundred.

Black bears reproduce faster than grizzlies and require less living space, so they can sustain a somewhat higher death rate. Even so, if hunting removes more than about 10 to 15 per cent of a black bear population each year, experience has shown that reproduction won't be enough to make up the difference and the number of bears will begin to fall.

Hunting, where it is allowed, is controlled by wildlife agencies. What cannot be so easily controlled is poaching, especially in areas where there are many backcountry roads and trails available for motorized vehicles. It only takes one or two individuals with hatred for bears and disdain for regulations to greatly increase the bear mortality rate when open roads and off-road vehicle trails provide good access.

Another factor that can lead to high death rates in bear populations is the presence of camps, dumps or permanent homes in bear country. Anywhere humans dwell, there will almost certainly be garbage, barbecues, livestock or other tempting sources of easy food. This kind of easy food, once a bear learns how to find it, is a one-way ticket to an early death.

Bear worms
If you're inclined to eat it, bear meat is fine-grained and rich. Some connoisseurs compare it to pork. And as was once the case with pork, it frequently conceals a deadly parasite, a small worm that causes trichinosis in humans.

Thorough cooking kills the *Trichinella* worm, but it can survive if the meat is cooked rare. Virtually every polar bear ever examined carried the tiny parasite, and at least three out of every four grizzlies. Its abundance in black bears varies from one area to another. Bears that are otherwise healthy have little trouble coexisting with the parasite, but it's fatal for humans.

The Great Bear Foundation

One of the world's leading bear conservation organizations, the Missoula-based Great Bear Foundation is involved in leading-edge programs to promote bear conservation around the world.

In 1994 the GBF sent a research crew to Russia to meet Russian conservationists and investigate the slaughter of brown bears by wealthy trophy hunters and by traffickers in bear parts. The international profile they continue to bring to this issue may help save one of the most productive bear populations left in the world.

Closer to home, the GBF has played an important role in support of the Valhalla Wilderness Society's efforts to protect the rare white bears of BC's Great Bear Wilderness. In Montana, recognizing that federally protected grizzlies kill domestic livestock, GBF for many years paid compensation to the ranchers to increase tolerance of the great bears.

The Great Bear Foundation publishes a twenty-page newspaper covering bear conservation issues from around the world. *Bear News* is widely acknowledged to be one of the most comprehensive and accurate sources of current bear information in the world.

The Great Bear Foundation
www.greatbear.org
PO Box 9383
802 East Front Street
Missoula, Montana, USA
59807-9383

406 829-9378
gbf@greatbear.org

ENDANGERED BEARS

Animal species go extinct naturally. But in the past century extinction rates worldwide have shot to almost unprecedented levels. Usually the problem is habitat loss from too much development, often combined with high mortality in the fragmented habitat that remains. More recently, global climate change has become a bigger threat, since even where habitat is protected, climate changes can severely damage vegetation, soils and water supplies.

The United States signed its Endangered Species Act into law in 1973 when it became obvious that without legal protection many plants and animals would continue the slide into extinction. The Act defines an endangered species as "any species which is in danger of extinction throughout all or a significant portion of its range." A threatened species is one which is likely to become endangered.

South of the 49th parallel, fewer than two thousand grizzly bears survive in the fragmented wildlands of Montana, Idaho, Washington and Wyoming. Many of these bears are isolated in island-like pockets of habitat surrounded by human development – what bear ecologist Wayne McCrory calls "islands of extinction." Because of the small number of bears and the fragmentation of their habitat, grizzlies are listed as an endangered species in the US.

Once a species has been listed under the ESA, the US Fish & Wildlife Service is required to come up with a recovery plan. No federal agency is allowed to do anything that might harm the species. Since most public land in the western US is under the control of federal agencies like the US Forest Service, the Bureau of Land Management and the National Parks Service, protection of grizzly bear habitat under the ESA can lead to restrictions on how westerners cut trees, graze cattle or enjoy recreation.

As a result, the ESA comes under frequent attack by libertarian politicians and states' rights advocates, who resent the influence of federal agencies and eastern voters on rural westerners. The ESA is seen as a symbol of uncaring outsiders who put animals before people. A grizzly might reply that with about three hundred million humans and fewer than two thousand grizzlies surviving in the continental US, there isn't a lot of evidence to support that charge.

In fact, horror stories about the impact of the ESA on the economic needs of ordinary Americans rarely stand up to scrutiny. Even in the Pacific Northwest, where the northern spotted owl, threatened with extinction by over-cutting of ancient rainforests, was listed under the ESA and immediately became a symbol of all that was wrong with the Act, most job losses in the forest industry have been caused by forest companies choosing to replace people with machines and cut forests faster than they can grow back. Conservationists point out that the two largest grizzly populations south of the 49th parallel – in the Greater Yellowstone and Northern Continental Divide Ecosystems – have both more than doubled since gaining protection. Along with other successes, like the restoration of bald eagles and wolves, they see the continuing recovery of grizzlies as proof of why America needs to retain, and strengthen, its Endangered Species Act.

Canada's 2002 Species at Risk Act, by comparison, is weak soup. It has yet to help any of Canada's many threatened and endangered species, and without some serious improvements it likely never will. The Act applies only on federal lands, such as military training areas, Indian reserves and national parks. Even on this small part of the western landscape, the Canadian legislation has proven to have enough bureaucratic loopholes to defer tangible action for years, while having no legislative teeth or fining provisions to ensure its enforcement.

If the increasingly fragmented and vulnerable grizzly bear populations of southern British Columbia and Alberta survive into the future, it will be in spite of Canada's current endangered species legislation, not because of it.

Nature needs half

The late twentieth century saw astronomic increases in the rate at which logging, dam-building, mining and other forms of development destroyed habitat for bears and other animals. The problem was most acute in poor

Third World countries where the World Bank financed exploitation schemes benefiting European and North American companies at the expense of indigenous peoples and their environments.

In 1983, in response to growing international concern, the United Nations established a World Commission on Environment and Development, chaired by Gro Harlem Brundtland, former prime minister of Norway.

One of the Brundtland Commission's recommendations when it submitted its final report in 1987 was that each nation should protect at least 12 per cent of its lands and waters as parks or ecological reserves, as insurance against the loss of biodiversity.

In response, Canada promised the world that it would set aside at least 12 per cent of its land base by 2000. Parks Canada, the federal parks agency, fell short of that goal, as did the province of Alberta. Alberta's "Special Places" initiative set aside some small patches of bear country, but left critical areas like the Castle and upper Oldman drainages and Swan Hills open for industrial development.

The province of British Columbia, on the other hand, more than doubled the area devoted to parks and protected areas. Some of BC's new large wilderness parks, such as the White Grizzly (Goat Range) Wilderness, Granby, Khutzeymateen and Tatshenshini, included productive and important bear habitat.

Harvey Locke argues that the failure of Canada to meet its 12 per cent goal masks a bigger problem: even 12 per cent is far too little if nature's diversity is to survive. Having helped found the visionary Yellowstone to Yukon Conservation Initiative (Y2Y) in the 1990s, Harvey joined other leading North American conservation thinkers to launch a much more ambitious conservation plan for the twentieth century.

"Nature Needs Half" is based on a quote from ecologist E.O. Wilson in his 2002 book *The Future of Life*. "Half the world for humanity, half for the rest of life, to make a planet both self-sustaining and pleasant." Conservation biologists are now working to ensure that at least half of Canada survives in its natural state as parks or other forms of protected area, while the rest is managed for other land uses in ways that still respect the needs of native vegetation and wildlife.

4

BEAR COUNTRY

THE BIG PICTURE

Late March, and storm wrack is piled high on Long Beach, south of Tofino.

The sky is grey, the air full of the smell of seaweed and salt; waves sweeping endlessly onshore from the Pacific Ocean break and race across the sands. Sand dollars and broken clam shells, kelp stringers and sodden bits of driftwood wash landward across the beach, then back toward the sea to lodge in new-washed sand, breaking the ripples of retreating waves into delicate patterns that vanish as each next wave hisses in.

A squabble of gulls huddle around the rotting carcass of a sea lion washed in by last night's high tide. Their keening calls echo lonely down the empty sands, then erupt into a chorus of protests as they lift into the offshore wind and wheel in a tangled circle to land on the sand a few yards away.

The black bear who startled the gulls with his sudden appearance from the salal at the edge of the beach ignores their bitter commentary as he follows his nose toward the stinking remains. He is three years old this spring and weighs twenty kilograms less than he did late in December, when he excavated his winter den beneath the roots of an uprooted Sitka spruce. The

Bears prefer lush greenery and diverse vegetation.

mouldering, fat-rich carcass will give him a big start on the task of rebuilding his weight.

As the bear begins to tear at the sea lion's swollen paunch, releasing a sudden stench of methane and rot, a wall of grey sweeps in across the breakers and up the beach. Icy rain pelts the impatient gulls and rattles the salal; treetops vanish into a slanting greyness.

Thousands of kilometres of Pacific Ocean stretch to the west, an unimaginable expanse of water spread beneath the sky. Water evaporated from that ocean and swept inland by humid weather systems is the source of the rain that drips from the feeding black bear's fur.

On the west slope of Vancouver Island, more than a metre and a half of rain falls each year, mostly during winter. The towering rain forests of Pacific Rim National Park and the coastal drainages of BC are products of abundant rainfall – those cathedral-like forests and the black bears that haunt them get first dibs on the moisture that billows inland from the Pacific each year.

Much of the moisture runs back to the ocean in rambunctious coastal rivers that fill yearly with salmon heading inland to spawn. Bears emerge from dripping forests to harvest this annual abundance of protein until the spawn is over; then they return to the lush greenery sustained by the same frequent rains that feed the salmon rivers.

Eastward, the storms are forced to rise again and again as they cross first the Coast Ranges, then the Selkirks and Purcells and finally the Rockies. Most of the mountain ranges trend southeast to northwest, almost perpendicular to the line of movement followed by the weather systems surging in from the southwest.

And so, in accordance with the laws of physics, each

mountain range intercepts its share of Pacific moisture and leaves the air masses a little drier and a little warmer as they continue to spill inland across the continent.

When those great weather systems break at length against the Rocky Mountains, the widest and highest mountain range of all, they have lost most of their moisture – yet still they retain enough to shed copious snow and rain on the high country of Yoho and Kootenay National Parks and up to 10 metres of snow each year on the Waputik, Wapta, Columbia, Brazeau and other icefields and glaciers of the Canadian Rockies.

Air is a fluid, like water; it flows along the lines of least resistance. The remains of the Pacific storms break like waves across the Continental Divide into Alberta and spill down the valleys of the Athabasca, Brazeau, North Saskatchewan, Bow and Oldman Rivers. Losing elevation, they gain warmth, and now, as warm, dry chinook winds, they sweep out onto the western edge of the Great Plains. The chinook winds are thirsty now, and they suck moisture from the grassland soils of the Alberta foothills and prairies.

East of the mountains, the Pacific Ocean's influence is weak. Great weather systems that slump down from the Arctic become more important here in winter, and warm humid systems sweep north from the Gulf of Mexico in summer. Icy temperatures and sparse but long-lasting snows are the rule across the prairies, aspen parkland and northern forests of Alberta, Saskatchewan and Manitoba in winter. Bears that rise too early here find no easy meals, only snow and hunger.

As the black bear gulps down hunks of well-cured sea lion in the sullen drizzle, the same storm is shedding snow on the high Coast Range north of Vancouver. Other black bears still doze there, beneath a metre or more of snow. They will not venture out of their dens for another month or so.

Farther east, the storm has not yet arrived in the Selkirk, Purcell and Rocky Mountains. It is late afternoon there, and bright spring sunshine slants down on the aging snowpack where it grips the steep lee slopes and leans out from the peaks in wind-sculpted cornices. As they have each late March and April for millennia, avalanches of sun-weakened snow thunder down gullies and lee slopes, following predictable paths between forested spurs. At the head of some avalanche paths, and in other high-elevation places where snow accumulates, grizzlies sleep curled up in snowbound dens. Near the base, beneath the hard accumulations of the snow slides, glacier lilies, spring beauty and other plants are quickening, life stirring in bulbs and buds and roots; they will begin to sprout as the snowbanks melt in another month or two, just in time to feed awakening bears.

Late March is still winter throughout most of BC and Alberta's high country. Beneath the blanketing snow, hundreds of black and grizzly bears lie asleep or stir sluggishly as rabbit-sized bear cubs, born only a month or two earlier, nurse hungrily and fatten on milk twice as rich as human or cow milk.

East of Lake Louise, however, pigeon-toed tracks in the crusty late-winter snow of the lower Bow valley plot the course of an old male grizzly bear who has wakened early. His worn teeth and an injured foreleg hindered his efforts to find food last fall, and now he is sick and weak, his inadequate winter fat supply long gone. He works his way along the railway line, head low, eyes dim, his nose seeking out grains of wheat spilled from train cars. He will die soon.

A few other bears have emerged along the eastern slopes of the Rockies, early risers looking for winter-killed elk and deer, but most bears on the chilly east side of the Continental Divide are still asleep, waiting for the warmth and greenery of spring before they venture out again into western Canada's bear country.

At the coarsest scale, then – as viewed perhaps from high above the Earth's surface – late March reveals four broad categories of bear country in western Canada:

Bear country

Temperate rainforest
Along the western rim of the continent and extending up the valleys of the major rivers, a broad band of temperate rainforest remains green and largely snow-free throughout most of the winter. Steep

streams and surging rivers pour out of the interior mountains through lush evergreen forests. Each year, great runs of salmon school at the mouths of those streams not blocked by dams or fouled by too much logging, then surge upstream to spawn in shallow headwaters. Winters are brief, the land is lush and the streams provide reliable seasonal supplies of high-energy food. This is bear paradise, and here some of Canada's largest black and – north of Vancouver Island – grizzly bears thrive. Inland from the coast, some interior rainforests are nearly as productive as the coastal ones.

Mountains and plateaus

Inland, the mountains and plateaus of BC's interior and the western edge of Alberta are buried under deep snows for four to seven months of each year. Bears still gather seasonally to eat salmon along some of the streams draining from distant headwaters, where there are no natural waterfalls or man-made dams to block the runs.

For the most part, however, black and grizzly bears

that dwell in the interior mountains and plateaus rely on vegetation, insects and the occasional large animal for food, travelling through the short summer from one seasonal food concentration to another. Much of the landscape is poor-quality bear habitat – continuous coniferous forest, rock, ice, human settlements – but pockets of abundance are found along stream bottoms, in burned and logged areas, on avalanche slopes and in the bands of interior rainforest that lie along the rainy sides of major mountain ranges. Bears generally have to wander widely across the mountain landscape, from one patch of high-quality habitat to another.

Prairie and parkland

East of the Rockies, winter snows are relatively light and a chronic scarcity of moisture restricts forests only to sheltered places – north-facing slopes out of the sun, high hilltops where temperatures are cooler and evaporation consequently lower, or well-watered stream bottoms. Here, in the prairie and parkland regions of North America's Great Plains, concentrations of grizzly bears

once inspired respect and fear among aboriginal people and white explorers alike. The bear country of the Great Plains, for the most part, is now devoid of any bears at all. A few pockets of grizzly and black bears hang on along the western edges of the plains, where ranching country and protected parks offer haven.

Northern forest
North of the prairies, aspen parkland gives way to the boreal forests of northeastern BC and northern Alberta, Saskatchewan and Manitoba. These northern forests are blanketed with snow throughout most of the winter, locked in a subarctic deep-freeze as black bears and – in the northern foothills and Alberta's Swan Hills region – a dwindling number of grizzlies sleep the cold season away. The northern forests of pine, aspen and spruce are a recently glaciated, rolling landscape of bogs, wetlands and twisting streams. Summer is short, hot and lush. Fires sweep the landscape each year, creating a complex mosaic of open shrub-lands, young forests and pockets

of older trees. Black bears are abundant in many parts of this northern mosaic because the diversity of vegetation and abundance of water in the landscape ensures them a bear-food smorgasbord during the snow-free season.

As March gives way to April, and the northern winter gradually surrenders to the first green rustlings of spring, western North America's bears emerge blinking into the light of another year. It is time again for the business of making a living in bear country.

Great Bear Rainforest

Princess Royal Island, 120 kilometres southeast of Prince Rupert, BC, is part of a complex of islands and mainland drainages that have the highest concentration of white Kermode bears anywhere in the world. As many as one out of every seven bears on the island is white – a gene pool so unique that in 1994 a consortium of German hunters who owned non-resident hunting rights to part of the island voluntarily agreed to stop hunting bears to protect it.

Western Canada's leading bear biologists and wilderness advocates began a campaign in the 1990s to have the island protected as part of a 265,000-hectare (655,000-acre) wilderness park where Moksgm'ol – the Tsimshian people's name for the rare Kermode – could continue to live untouched by twentieth-century industrial development. Their proposed sanctuary would include Swindle, Campania and Princess Royal Islands and three large watersheds on the mainland, making it large enough to protect not just the bear population but also the ancestral homeland of the Kitasoo people, and

Most of the world's rare white Kermode bears live in the Great Bear Rainforest.

more spawning salmon than all other parks and protected areas in BC combined.

During the early 1990s, biologists Wayne McCrory and Erica Mallam, outfitter Tom Ellison and editor Bart Robinson became aware of plans to open up Princess Royal and other, adjacent areas for logging. They joined forces with Gitga'at and Kitasoo First Nations to mobilize support for protecting the area. Charlie Russell – who was working then as a wilderness guide for Tom Ellison – published *Spirit Bear* in 1994. The book helped draw the world's attention to the once-remote rainforests just as logging companies began mobilizing to log them

Following a successful campaign to protect Clayoquot Sound from large-scale clear-cutting, environmental groups coined the name "Great Bear Rainforest" for a much larger area that included the original park proposal. They launched an international campaign in 1997 for its protection. One of their most effective tactics was to target forest companies through their customers, getting large consumer outlets to cancel orders for wood or paper from companies that were logging bear habitat.

Following government-sponsored negotiations that involved First Nations, logging companies, environmentalists, local communities and other stakeholders, a planning committee recommended in 2004 that a third of the Great Bear Rainforest – about fourteen thousand square kilometres – should receive permanent protection. Even this ambitious proposal was a compromise, since ecosystem scientists advising the group had suggested protecting an area twice as large. The remainder of the Great Bear Rainforest, the group said, should be managed under restrictive new rules for logging that would protect ecosystem health.

The BC government accepted the recommendations in 2006. It banned loggers from a third of the area, including most of Princess Royal Island. The government also promised to identify a number of conservation reserves for grizzly bears and to establish new, ecosystem-based forestry guidelines for the rest of the area by 2009. They have yet to keep either promise.

The Great Bear Rainforest accord was one of the largest conservation success stories in the history of North America's bear country, even if it has not yet been fully implemented.

But conservation success is sometimes fleeting. A new threat – Enbridge's proposed Northern Gateway pipeline from Alberta's tar sands to tankers in Kitimat

- may damage food supplies and habitat for bears. If approved, the pipeline will carry raw bitumen through earthquake zones and landslide-prone slopes above salmon streams to tankers that must then thread their way past the rocky shorelines of once-remote bear islands.

Whiteout

"The number one threat to grizzly bears today is those white areas on the map that represent private lands. All the human activity going on down there will negate anything we can hope to do for grizzlies on public lands, if we don't find a way to bring rampant development under control.

"The next fifteen years are critical. The Highway 3 corridor in Alberta and BC has the potential to cut off US grizzly populations completely. That's a really frightening possibility with large carnivore populations fracturing as they already are in the northern US Rockies. There are incredible rates of development, and the rate is not slowing down – it's accelerating. Most people aren't aware of the impact of what's happening in the valleys on grizzlies and other species."

—Chris Servheen, coordinator of the
US Grizzly Recovery Team

Wayne McCrory, bear ecologist

Wayne McCrory says he grew up in BC "at a time when there were still prospectors, outfitters, bears and all

Wayne McCrory and cameraman Michio Hoshino.

those frontier sorts of things – Winchester rifles and all that. I grew up with bears and I guess I developed an early affinity for them. I've always been fascinated by them."

In the early 1960s, McCrory was about to embark on a career as a mining engineer "when I found out there was such a thing as a wildlife biologist." He changed course, choosing to study bears in Jasper and Glacier National Parks instead of carving minerals out of their habitat elsewhere.

McCrory has studied grizzly and black bears in almost every part of BC and western Alberta and is widely recognized as one of Canada's leading authorities on bear ecology. It is no coincidence that he is also a determined and successful advocate for wilderness protection.

In 1975 McCrory teamed up with his sister Colleen and other wildlands advocates to form the Valhalla Wilderness Society. The original focus of the organization was to secure protection for the rugged mountains and forests of the Valhalla Range, west of Slocan Lake. Their campaign paid off in 1983 and was followed by successful campaigns to protect the Khutzeymateen watershed in 1992 and the White Grizzly Wilderness in 1995. "Every one of those is a critical rainforest bear area," says McCrory, "and together they total just under half a million acres [202,300 hectares]."

McCrory, however, is far from ready to rest on his laurels. He continues to alternate between his role as a professional biologist, applying the best possible science to grizzly conservation issues as objectively as possible, and his continuing conservation advocacy work with the Valhalla Society.

"Only 6 per cent of coastal temperate rainforest and 7.3 per cent of interior temperate rainforest has been protected so far," he pointed out in the 1990s. "That means that industry gets well over 90 per cent to clearcut." McCrory said that parks and protected areas risk becoming islands of extinction if they are not connected by landscapes containing healthy, secure habitat for grizzly bears. However, he says, that is not what was happening.

"On the plus side, we've got a large number of new parks. On the negative side, they're logging the hell out of the landscape in between. The provincial government promotes its new Forest Practices Code as the way it's ensuring logging won't harm wildlife. But there are no grizzly bear habitat guidelines in the Forest Practices Code, just as there are no guidelines for caribou or other species that need a large amount of unlogged forest. When the guidelines were being formulated, the government insisted that they couldn't result in any substantial reduction in the annual allowable cut, so they don't deal with animals like grizzlies."

McCrory subsequently went on to play a key role in helping persuade the BC government to protect most of the Great Bear Rainforest on the central BC coast in 2006. More than one-third of this 250,000-hectare coastal ecosystem was protected in parks, and most of the rest was to be spared from clear-cut logging and roads that put bears at risk by ruining salmon streams and exposing bears to poaching. The Great Bear Rainforest sustains most of the world's population of white-phase (Kermode) black bears, as well as many grizzlies. In combination with Gwaii Haanas National Park, Tweedsmuir Provincial Park and the recently established Kitlope Provincial Park, the area provides an almost continuous belt of wilderness bear habitat stretching from the Pacific Ocean into the BC interior.

Bears need space

Parks just aren't enough to ensure that grizzly bears will have a future.

Waterton Lakes National Park, for example, is barely a third the size of a single male grizzly's home range. Even Jasper National Park – fifteen times the size of tiny Waterton – has few grizzly bears that spend their whole lives in the park. A grizzly bear conservation strategy released by the BC government in 1995 states: "Existing protected areas in themselves ... may not be adequate for grizzly bear conservation for a number of reasons:

1. They are not sufficiently large.

2. They do not, for the most part, contain prime grizzly bear habitat or all of the ecological requirements of a grizzly bear population.

3. Many were ... initially established ... to capture scenic or recreational wilderness values."

Grizzly sanctuary

In British Columbia, an NDP government brought one of that province's many long-running environmental battles to a happy conclusion in 1994 when it announced that the rugged Khutzeymateen River valley, forty kilometres north of Prince Rupert, had been set aside as Canada's first sanctuary for grizzly bears. Today it includes a 443-square-kilometre Class A provincial park surrounded by more than three thousand square kilometres of landscape in which bear hunting is no longer permitted.

The sanctuary didn't come easily. It took a decade-long media campaign and lobbying action by biologists, wilderness advocates and environmentalists to persuade the BC government to let the remote watershed's population of fifty or so grizzlies live in peace. Long recommended as an ecological reserve because of its importance to grizzlies, salmon and old-growth forest stands, the valley was thrown open for clear-cut logging in 1986. By 1988 its fate seemed sealed, but the environmental coalition turned up the heat by taking the battle to save the valley into the international arena.

Ultimately it was an election that saved the Khutzeymateen. With the election of a new government committed to resolving BC's land use conflicts fairly and rationally, rather than exclusively in the interests of the industrial sector, it was only a matter of time before the Khutzeymateen's obvious ecological values led to its protection.

Charlie Russell still shakes his head when he thinks of how close the bears came to losing their home place: "It seems remarkable to me that it would have taken so long to set aside a sanctuary for these animals that represent the essence of our country."

Khutzeymateen Estuary.

The Khutzeymateen River drains the glaciers and rugged headwater valleys of BC's Kitimat Range, flowing between steep valley walls clothed with temperate rain forest to spill its waters into a lush estuary at the inland end of a narrow fjord. *Khutzeymateen* is a Tsimshian word that translates, roughly, to "sheltered place of fish and bears."

It's the annual rendezvous of fish and bears that has given the place its fame. Each August, schools of chinook, chum, coho and pink salmon that have been massing in the fjord begin their annual spawning run through the estuary and up the river. Grizzly bears, treading bear trails so ancient that they are permanently worn into the mossy forest floor, converge upon the river mouth to feast on salmon.

Some of these bears weigh more than four hundred kilograms, their size attesting to the richness of their coastal environment and the importance of salmon to their diet. In a province where many salmon runs have been lost or damaged by clear-cut logging that deposits eroded silt in spawning beds or causes floods that scour away spawning gravels, and where other salmon runs are gone forever because of hydropower dams, the Khutzeymateen's salmon still return each summer to a pristine watershed.

Now that the area is a grizzly sanctuary, its salmon and grizzlies are assured a secure habitat well into the future. But the battle to save the valley has also awakened public interest in visiting it, and that brings its own risks. In other parks and protected areas where humans have recreational access to grizzly habitat, history has shown that the bears come up the losers.

Environmental groups involved in publicizing the area anticipated the potential for problems rather than waiting for them to arise, and developed a carefully controlled, water-based bear viewing program. When the government finally gave the Khutzeymateen formal protection, it also adopted this conservative viewing program.

"Even while we were lobbying for protection, we studied the three Alaska bear areas – Pack Creek, Katmai and McNeil River Falls – to find out what worked and what didn't," says Wayne McCrory, who later helped the provincial government develop its management plan for the area. "Pack Creek was the most similar to Khutzeymateen. The plan has some provision for limited guiding by park rangers so that the non-paying public would have some opportunities, but there is no uncontrolled public access."

Charlie Russell guided small groups of naturalists and bear enthusiasts into the estuary for several years. Even now, with its higher profile as a sanctuary, Russell says, "There's very few people come in on their own, and the ones that do aren't allowed to go into the estuary on their own. They have to have a guide with them. Up to now there hasn't been one for the general public, so the only visitors are the ones who can book space with a licensed tour company."

Ocean Light, the boat out of which Russell operated, held eight people. *SunChaser*, the other tour boat in the area, held four. "So twelve people is about the maximum per day that's allowed into the area, and that's only for about one month of the year when it's feasible. The rest of the year the bears are dispersed up the valley and in the mountains.

"The country is rugged, and the areas where they hang out during other months are not open to the public. There's no trails, and the river is blocked by logjams. So they have it very secluded there."

Guided visitors to the sanctuary sleep offshore on boats to minimize any risk of grizzlies coming to associate humans with food or waste. Russell, who no longer guides in the area, says that visitors appreciate the chance to learn from trained guides: "I find that guiding people bear-watching, they really want to know how to do it. Most people have got a long way from knowing etiquette in the wild and what our actions do to bears and the possibilities of getting in trouble. People really seem to appreciate getting direction in that way."

Wayne McCrory, Erica Mallan and the many others who fought hard to save Khutzeymateen's grizzlies from industrial development now hope to make this one place where bears can remain unspoiled by contact with humans, but a limited number of people can still visit, and learn from, the annual encounter between salmon and bear in the heart of a spectacular wilderness.

5
BLACK BEAR

Ursus americanus

Curiosity not only killed the cat, it often proves disastrous for black bears. Intelligent, curious, perpetually hungry, black bears quickly learn to exploit human sloppiness in their endless quest for energy-rich foods. As a result, their foraging frequently brings them into conflict with humans, who rarely tolerate the bears or blame themselves.

Black bears once ranged throughout the forested parts of North America, including most of the eastern half of the continent. They rely on trees for security, climbing them to escape attacks by other bears. The more open landscapes of the great plains, the high mountains and the Arctic tundra were largely out of bounds for them, both because their habitat needs confined them to forested or partly forested areas, and because grizzly bears, polar bears or both occupied the open country and aggressively hunted their smaller relatives.

Black bears thrive best in forests dense with greenery.

Black bear facts

Length	1.2–1.9 m (3.7–6.0 ft.)
Weight	90–250 kg (200–600 lb.)
Description	Black, brown, cinnamon; rarely greyish-blue or ivory white. Appear taller at the hind end than the front; have large round ears and a long nose.
Reproduction	First breed at 3–5 years of age; have 1–4 cubs every two or more years.
Lifespan	20 years in the wild; some individuals have lived more than 30 years.
Diet	Plants, insects, meat.
Distribution	Live in forested parts of North America, but have been extirpated from parts of the central and eastern United States.

Black bear diet

Paul Paquet studied black bears in Manitoba's Riding Mountain National Park during the late 1980s. He examined the contents of 212 bear scats and 24 stomachs, the kind of undertaking that should be enough to discourage anyone from considering a career in wildlife biology.

Many of the Riding Mountain bears fed regularly at the park's garbage dump, but garbage actually showed up in only 3 per cent of the scats and stomachs examined. Remains of mammals and birds were rare, too, but Paquet noted three cases of black bears attacking and killing elk calves during the course of his study.

A black bear feeds on poplar buds in early spring.

Food type	Percentage of samples
Vegetable matter	100
Invertebrates (ants, other insects etc.)	52
Garbage and debris	3
Mammals and birds	3
Agricultural crops	5

Bears concentrated on different foods as the seasons changed:

Spring	grasses, legumes, other herbs
Summer	insects, berries, grasses
Fall	acorns, berries, agricultural crops like oats

Farther west, a food habits study of black bears in the Cold Lake area of Alberta found a similar pattern. In this boreal forest area, however, blueberries were far more important and acorns weren't, since oak trees are rare between southern Manitoba and the Pacific coast.

In the Alberta Rockies, research has revealed a similar pattern of changing seasonal foods, but again with different plant species being favoured because of the different vegetation and habitats:

Early spring	forbs, bearberry, horsetail, carrion
Late spring	cow parsnip, forbs, ants, carrion
Summer	ants, buffalo berry, forbs
Late summer	raspberry, buffalo berry, wasps
Fall	bearberry, bog cranberry, carrion

When Europeans arrived in North America, they set to work clearing openings in the great eastern forests for both farming and timber. The resulting patchwork quilt of habitats greatly improved habitat quality for the North American black bear, which also found rich new food sources in the settlers' crops, domestic livestock, chicken coops and beehives. It was a double-edged sword: more ways to dine, and more ways to die.

Bears were hunted for food, trapped and shot to protect farms and crops and were killed out of fear. As settlement intensified and spread west across the continent, black bears began to vanish from many parts of their former range.

Black bears today occupy barely half of their historical North American range. They are extremely rare today in Ohio, Kentucky, Illinois and Alabama, where they once were abundant. Black bear populations in most of southern Ontario, Quebec and the Maritimes are confined to land that hasn't been pre-empted for agriculture. All across Canada where forest land is inter-fingered with farmland, black bears suffer high mortality. They sustain their populations mostly through the immigration of young bears dispersing from more remote areas.

In western Canada, however, the distribution of black bears is little changed from what it was when the flood of European settlement first swept west across the plains. Island populations of black bears still occupy Manitoba's Riding Mountain area and Saskatchewan's Duck Mountains, and the bears remain widespread and locally common throughout the northern forests and the forested valleys of the western mountains. The black bear remains the best-known and most frequently seen of the three species of native North American bears.

When is a black bear white?

Ghost-like, surreally beautiful and rare, the Kermode, or spirit bear, haunts the coastal rainforests near Terrace, on Princess Royal Island and in a few other parts of British Columbia.

Once considered a unique species, the Kermode came to be considered a subspecies of the black bear. More recently, scientists have determined that the Kermode isn't even a subspecies; spirit bears theoretically can turn up anywhere there are black bears. Genetic research has shown the ghost bear to be a rare colour phase that results when two normal black bears, each with the same recessive gene, breed together. Some black bear litters contain both black and white cubs since only cubs that receive the gene from both parents will develop white fur.

The Kermode is a rare white variant of the black bear.

Charlie Russell, whose *Spirit Bear* is a fascinating book on the Kermodes of Princess Royal Island, has even seen a white-phase "Kermode" grizzly in Waterton Lakes National Park in Alberta. Wayne McCrory points out that a rare white colour phase of the grizzly is sometimes seen in the West Kootenays region of BC; he describes these bears as having Siamese-cat-like faces, white bodies and black legs.

Kermode bears are seen regularly only in the few bear populations where a high proportion of individuals carry the Kermode gene. Only two hundred or so are believed to exist in the wild, even though more than 10 per cent of the black bears on Princess Royal Island and nearby islands and mainland drainages carry the gene.

BC declared the Kermode bear its provincial mammal in 2006. Three years later, the government set aside two million hectares of the Great Bear Rainforest as protected habitat for the spirit bears.

"I will perish of disappointment..."

William Hornaday, the ambitious director of the New York Zoological Society, really wanted a white bear for his zoo. Having heard from a New York fur trader of the existence of the rare white bear in 1900, he set to work trying to find out where it came from. His investigations led him, at length, to a fur dealer in Port Essington, BC. The dealer wrote Hornaday that he regularly received skins of ivory-coloured bears from First Nations hunters in "... the district south of the Skeena River, sometimes as far south as Rivers Inlet."

Hornaday solicited the help of the BC Provincial Museum to help him get hold of a live specimen. When, in 1904, the museum took delivery of two dead cubs, Hornaday promptly arranged for the new species of white bear to be officially named *Ursus kermodei* after the new curator of the Provincial Museum, Francis Kermode. It appears Hornaday hoped that, through bestowing this honour on the thirty-year-old Kermode, Hornaday would be assured of the young curator's cooperation. If so, his hopes were in vain.

Kermode finally managed to obtain a live white bear in 1924 when the BC Game Conservation Board seized a cub from a black marketeer who was trying to smuggle the little bear into the US. Hornaday wrote to Kermode, saying, "If we don't get that cub, I will perish of disappointment."

He didn't get it. Instead, the poor animal spent the next twenty-two years in a cramped pen in Victoria's Beacon Hill Park, dying of old age in 1948.

Hornaday's regret was short-lived in any case. After a prominent taxonomist from the University of California determined, in 1928, that the Kermode bear was only a colour phase of the American black bear, and not a new species as Hornaday had originally believed, the zoologist lost interest in his dream of putting BC's white bears on display in New York City.

Bears of many colours
A black bear can be blue, brown, blonde, white or black. This leads to no lack of confusion and has led to suggestions from some biologists that the black bear should be renamed the American bear or some other name that avoids any mention of colour at all.

Brown or cinnamon bears are common in the Rocky Mountains.

The name, and the confusion, originated when Europeans explorers first ventured inland from the Atlantic coast. The bears they encountered in the lush deciduous forests were black, because that colour phase predominates in eastern North America. The name "black bear" was well-established by the time settlers, spreading west across the continent, began to run into brown variants of *Ursus americanus.*

Montana bear biologist Charles Jonkel speculates that the prevalence of one colour or another in different parts of the black bear's range may relate to environmental variations. Brown-phase bears are quite common in the Rocky Mountains and the drier regions of western North America, where bears often feed on open, south-facing slopes early in the spring. Jonkel has observed that light-phase bears seem to feed on these exposed habitats longer than black ones, perhaps because they don't heat up as rapidly in the intense spring sunshine. Over the course of many bear generations, it may be that brown bears, on average, tend to thrive more than black ones in those environments.

Every year, many visitors to the western national parks mistake brown-phase black bears for grizzly bears. Their confusion isn't helped any by the fact that many grizzly bears are not grizzled: they can range in colour from blonde to almost black too, although grizzlies show far less variability than black bears do.

Blue (glacier) and white (Kermode) colour phases also turn up in black bears that live in some parts of western BC and southwestern Alaska. Both of these colours result from the combination of a recessive gene from the mother and the same recessive gene in the father. The odds of this happening depend on how many bears in the population carry the recessive gene. If only one parent contributes the gene to its offspring, then the cub will be normal-coloured. Two normal-coloured parents, if they both have the gene, can produce a white or blue offspring.

Blue-phase black bears – actually a pale slate colour – are now very rare, possibly because of selective predation during the late 1800s and early 1900s, when trophy hunters sought the novelty of killing the rare "glacier" bears. By selecting only the blue bears, hunters likely reduced the number of bears in the population that carried the unusual gene.

BLACK BEAR HABITAT

Black bears are forest bears, but they prefer forests with holes in them. Dense forest that's short on shrubbery or other understorey vegetation is of little value to bears except for shelter. The most valuable habitats are those where the tree canopy is sparse or patchy enough that sunlight can reach the forest floor.

Sunlight is the energy source that plants use for growth. A dense tree canopy can intercept so much sunlight that little reaches the forest floor. Few plants, other than mosses and ferns, can grow in the shadowed depths of such a forest.

Where forests have natural openings in their canopies, however, a dense mass of greenery generally results. Bears are vegetarians for the most part, and these green openings in the forest are like salad bars for them. In old-growth forests, aging trees that topple over allow the sun to penetrate to the forest floor and create green openings for black bears, and the rotting trunks of the fallen giants eventually become rich sources of ants, termites and other insect life.

River floodplains also provide excellent black bear habitat. Spring floods knock over old trees and create new green openings. The same floods often spread silt into low places and leave them saturated well into the summer, creating ideal growing conditions for sedges, horsetails and other prime food plants. Frogs, salamanders, fish and bird nests are also common on floodplains. Added all together, the various sources of bear food make floodplains exceptionally valuable habitat for black bears.

Overleaf: A mother black bear leads her cubs across a beaver dam.

Forest openings can also occur on a grand scale when wildfire roars across the landscape after a lightning storm or downwind from an untended campfire. In the aftermath of fires, scattered patches of living trees alternate with large tracts of blackened snags. No longer obscured by tree foliage, the soil soon erupts with greenery, and over the next several years ants and other insects invade the wood of the dead trees. Again, all the elements that add up to happy bears come together in the wake of a forest fire. In fact, according to the University of Calgary's Stephen Herrero and many other bear experts, our twentieth-century success at putting out forest fires has resulted in the gradual deterioration of bear habitat in many areas. National parks and other areas are now faced with the need to restore fire to the landscape, either by letting natural fires burn or by setting prescribed fires that can be controlled safely.

Another, more problematic form of forest opening results when humans clear off the trees for agriculture. Agricultural crops – particularly oats and other grains – are excellent bear food. In some areas, consequently, black bears can cause extensive crop damage. Many beekeepers are plagued by black bears that can't resist the unequalled richness of a feast of honey and young bees. Some ranchers leave the carcasses of dead sheep and cows out on the range rather than disposing of them properly, giving black bears a taste for mutton and beef. Sheep and young cows have no brains when it comes to avoiding predators, so black bear depredations on livestock can become an ongoing problem for some ranchers. Most successful ranchers, however, have long ago found solutions to bear conflicts. Electric fencing, the use of guardian animals and simple changes in pasture management can eliminate or greatly reduce problems with bears.

When agriculture or recreational cabins or second homes invade the forested habitat of black bears, the death rate of bears always increases. Roads built for logging, mining or other purposes also reduce the value of black bear habitat by exposing bears to increased hunting pressure, poaching and collisions with motor vehicles.

Smokey the Bear
"Remember! Only <u>you</u> can prevent forest fires."

The bear with the ranger hat and shovel has been sternly issuing the same warning to Americans for more than half a century. Finding someone who hasn't heard of Smokey the Bear is like trying to find someone who hasn't eaten oatmeal porridge. Generations of North American children have grown up with Smokey's propaganda echoing in their subconscious, believing forest fires to be environmental disasters rather than life-giving natural processes.

Smokey was born in 1944, part of a public relations campaign to encourage Americans to take better care of their fires. US Forest Service officials – concerned with ensuring that as many trees as possible grew up to become two-by-fours – were convinced that most of the fires ignited each year were caused by human carelessness. They developed a cartoon mascot to take that message into the woods on their behalf.

In 1950, fire fighters in New Mexico's Lincoln National Forest found an abandoned bear cub. A photograph of the tiny bear licking the face of a little girl appeared in newspapers across the United States, and the rescued cub was quickly christened Smokey, after "Smokey" Joe Martin, a legendary New York City fire chief.

Smokey the real bear grew old and died in a zoo in Washington, DC. He was brought home to Capitan, New Mexico, and buried beneath a plaque, one of the few black bears in history to receive a funeral of sorts. His grave is visited by thousands of people each year.

Smokey the poster bear continues to live on, warning new generations of campers each year of their responsibility to keep forests safe from fire, if not from chainsaws. As a good public servant, Smokey no doubt keeps his personal opinion to himself.

Real black bears, after all, vastly prefer burned areas to mature forests or clear-cuts.

Bears like honey

The worst thing Winnie the Pooh had to worry about when his appetite for honey got the better of him was the possibility of getting the honey jar stuck on his head. For real-life black bears, a taste for honey can be a one-way ticket to the boneyard.

There is a long history of conflict between bears and farmers in the honey-producing areas of BC and Alberta's Peace River region as well as the agricultural fringe areas along the Rocky Mountain foothills and in northern parts of the Prairie provinces.

Wildlife regulations in the western provinces treat black bears as agricultural nuisances that farmers are allowed to kill on sight. Farmers and beekeepers used to do this with such regularity that honey farming became a perpetual drain on black bear populations in the 1970s. Looking at it from the farmers' point of view, black bears were a perpetual drain on honey production that they couldn't afford to ignore.

Electric fencing is the solution of choice to the problem of bears and honey, since it protects both. Inexpensive solar-powered electric fencing systems became available in the 1980s. In areas where there used to be chronic conflicts between bears and beehives, most bee farmers have now fenced their bee yards. Few bears will touch a wet nose to a hot wire more than once.

FAMILY LIFE

A newborn black bear is little larger than a hamster. Blind and naked at birth, young black bears spend their first three or four months of life curled up in a den with their hibernating mother. The den is most likely to be a short tunnel that their mother dug out the previous fall, but some black bears den in the hollow interiors of very old trees, in caves, under wind-thrown trees, under summer cottages or even in culverts.

Bear milk is considerably richer in fat than human milk, so the black bear cubs grow rapidly during their time in the den. By the time they follow their mother out into the sunshine in April, most cubs have grown to the size of a housecat. Long-legged and awkward, bear cubs approach the adventure of life with boundless curiosity and playfulness. Most black bear families consist of only two cubs, but litters of three or four are not unusual.

The cubs stay close to their mother, especially during their first year of life. Unlike the larger grizzly, black bear cubs instinctively bolt for the nearest tree when danger threatens, climbing high into the branches while their mother takes a defensive position at the base. Female black bears are rarely as aggressive as grizzlies when it comes to defending their cubs. Biologists speculate that this is because there is no need for extreme aggression in light of the tree-climbing defence strategy of black bear cubs. Attacking another bear, a wolf or a human is a dangerous undertaking for a bear, one that it will avoid if possible.

A black bear cub climbs a tree.

Nonetheless, female black bears will take that risk if surprised in open terrain where there is no tree nearby, or if they find themselves separated from their cubs by another animal that they perceive to be a threat.

Black bear cubs remain with their mother for one to two years, learning how to seek out and forage on the diversity of foods that black bears rely upon through the seasons. Bears learn both from observation and from experimentation. Mother black bears provide plenty of opportunity for observation, and are there to supervise and discipline the cubs when their curiosity or experimentation gets out of hand or puts them in danger.

Young black bears separate from their mothers during their second or third spring. Some, especially males, may wander quite widely. It's often these dispersing juveniles that kill chickens or livestock, wander into campgrounds or otherwise come into conflict with humans. This is partly a result of their inexperience and curiosity, but it may also relate to the fact that young bears need to avoid attacks by older males. To do so, they frequently end up using marginal habitat where the chance of encountering a mature bear is lowest. Human settlements and recreational areas may attract young bears partly because older animals usually avoid such areas.

BLACK BEAR SOCIETY

If you go down to the woods today, don't expect to find a teddy bears' picnic.

Bears rarely spend much time in one another's company. Even though they spend most of their time alone, however, there is still a complex social system in black bear country. Unlike other animals that feed on vegetation, bears have relatively inefficient digestive systems. As a result, they leave evidence of their passing at frequent intervals in the form of large, smelly droppings that serve to advise other bears of their presence. Although black bears don't defend clearly defined territories, most live within a distinct home range and tend to steer clear of other bears except when food is concentrated and abundant.

Rarely, bears will fight, sometimes to the death, to assert dominance. More frequently, bears establish rank by threatening one another, displaying the size of their body, or engaging in brief skirmishes. Frequently, a smaller bear will simply flee at the sight of a larger one.

Black bears sometimes gather in larger numbers when food is abundant. At garbage dumps or salmon spawning runs, congregations of black bears result in many passive threat displays and other subtle interactions, but although the dominance structure of the bear society is maintained, the abundance of food generally results in a much higher degree of tolerance for one another. The bears still have a personal space that they defend, but in the presence of a rich food source that space becomes quite small. It's not quite a picnic, but it's a gathering of animals who know one another and understand their own place in the social hierarchy.

Bruno was here
Bear "mark" or "rub" trees appear to serve a social function along the lines of leaving one's calling card. Some bear trees adjacent to heavily used trails are used again and again. Both black and grizzly bears exhibit the same

A bear tree, peeled for its sapwood.

behaviour, raking the bark with their claws or backing up against the tree to rub their backs on it. A lot of the use of bear trees seems to coincide with the approach of mating season, and it may be that bear trees help dominant males warn off competitors and stimulate females to become receptive to breeding.

Another kind of bear tree results when a black bear grips the bark at the base of the tree and pulls back, peeling a long, triangular strip from the tree. This behaviour has nothing to do with communicating with other bears – it's a way of feeding that appears unique to black bears. Black bears eat the sap-engorged inner wood in spring, often girdling several trees in one location. This sometimes kills the trees, inadvertently providing future meals. As the dead trees decompose, they turn into ant habitat.

Where bears girdle many young trees each spring, the habit makes them unpopular with the forest industry. For many years, some logging companies hired professional hunters to kill black bears. More recently, some have introduced artificial feeding programs to provide bears with an different food source during the short period each year when sapwood is palatable.

Spare that bear?

"We lost two calves to a black bear the summer of 1995. What had happened was we moved our cows and calves a month earlier than usual to a quarter up on the ridge, because of all the wet and flooding that year. It seemed like the cattle, the wildlife and everything was acting weird because of the flooding, and what was different was that I didn't get a chance to check that quarter out in advance like I normally would do.

"Bev and I went up to the dugout a few days later to check the cows and we saw on the ground this little calf and his guts were out. I'd never seen anything like this before because the last time a bear killed a calf all I found was the ear tag.

"I didn't have a rifle with me, so I drug him off into the bush and said, 'We'll have to come back after we've got the cows and shoot the little guy,' because he was still alive but way too badly tore up to be sewed back up. When I came back later, he'd died, so instead of

Keith Everts.

dragging off the carcass I left it there so we'd see if it was a predator. Because since I manage those cows, I have to know what's going on.

"I came back the next morning and found no sign of a predator coming back. The carcass was still there. I went on up the ridge by a big fir tree and went around the corner ... and there's another dead calf. This one had his hide peeled back just like a banana. And I look and there's the bear scat and the bear tracks.

"I called Fish and Wildlife and got the local officer, and he called in their bear specialist guy – I called him Rambo. When they arrived we went to the other side of the ridge and right away Rambo gets out and he's got his rifle ready; he's on a hunt, eh? We got ready to head up,

Bears rarely bother cattle pastured in bear country.

and he says, 'No, no, everybody stay behind me, nobody should be going in there that doesn't have to if there's a bear,' and I'm saying, 'I've already been all the way up; hey, I'll show you the tracks.'

"When we got there we looked at the hide and then he found the tracks, and he said it was a black bear. Then I went back and showed him the other one too. Once they'd skinned it then I could see the claw marks where he'd swatted it.

"They explained to me that once he's eaten calves he'll probably continue on and they'd have to trap him. They wanted to put the trap on the top of the ridge, and we had to get permission from my neighbour. I took the one officer but not Rambo, and [the neighbour] said okay.

"So they set the trap and Perry called me that night and he said, 'Geez, I forgot to ask you: when we kill the bear can we just leave it there?'

"I hadn't realized they were going to kill the bear. And now I'm feeling like an asshole, because I didn't want this bear to get killed. I thought we were just going to move it somewhere. But I'd made the complaint and now they had to follow it through. So I said, 'You definitely can't shoot it and leave it there, and don't tell my neighbour,' because I knew she wouldn't go for that.

"So anyway, I came back here and I told that to our family. And we moved cows. We made that decision.

"They never got her. She ended up to be a sow with two cubs and she lived on our ridge all summer. She's probably the biggest sow I've ever seen.

"We saw her several times, and we'd watch her. And yet, we have a lot of cows here too, and she never bothered them anymore. I think it was the flooding ... and my management, because I'd moved in there earlier than normal.

"And here, with Rambo and all, it was like everything was the bear's fault. I mean, sometimes you have to kill these bears, but I felt really bad because it wasn't all the bear's fault. It was nature, it was my management, and all these other factors. It's funny, because when we moved the cows we only went over one quarter section, and that was all it took."

—Keith Everts, Alberta rancher

BLACK BEARS THROUGH THE SEASONS

Black bears use a patchwork of habitats through the year, concentrating on different food sources as they come into season. A bear's knowledge of its home range is detailed and specific, because bears can't afford to waste too much energy in their annual race to gain weight before hibernation.

Black bears hibernate in a wide variety of places. Some dig dens or hollow out beds beneath the uprooted branches of wind-thrown trees. Bears in BC's rainforests often den in old-growth stands, where they can curl up inside hollowed-out old red cedars. In many areas black bears will spend the winter in culverts beneath roads, or in crawl spaces under isolated buildings. Where trees are large enough, black bears will even den in cavities high above the ground.

Black bears emerge from their dens as early as late February or March in low-elevation areas near the Pacific coast, to as late as mid-April in the Rocky Mountains and boreal forests. Early spring is a hungry time because little vegetation has sprouted. Bears usually continue to lose weight until well into June.

In early spring, black bears spend a lot of time on sun-warmed south-facing slopes, where they can find overwintered bearberries or scavenge for winter-killed deer and moose. The first green grasses and sedges often sprout right at the edges of streams or in open wetland meadows, so these areas also attract black bears early in spring.

Summer finds black bears focusing on pockets of greenery wherever these may be found – in wet meadows along creeks and rivers, on avalanche slopes, in aspen forests or along the edges of marshes.

As summer progresses, black bears may spend a significant amount of time grubbing ants and beetle larvae out of fallen logs. Late in July or early in August, with the first ripe blueberries, raspberries or other berries, black bears tend to focus all their efforts on exploiting this high-energy food source.

Fall is a critical time for black bears, as the race to fatten enough to survive the long winter goes into its final leg. As the berry crop succumbs to the first heavy frost, however, food supplies begin to dwindle. Spawning fish are important wherever there are reliable annual concentrations. Coastal black bears in particular hunt salmon during the annual spawning runs. Ripe fruit is hard for food-obsessed autumn bears to resist, and many end up in trouble when homeowners leave their crabapple and apple trees unpicked.

Elsewhere, black bears again concentrate on the late greenery that often persists near water, and wander widely looking for gut piles and wounded animals left behind by hunters. It seems likely that fall big game hunting seasons play a valuable role in giving modern black bears a reliable source of high-quality food in the last few weeks before they have to den up.

Black bears retire to their winter dens early in November as snow begins to accumulate or, in coastal areas, winter rains begin in earnest.

THREATS TO BLACK BEARS

Wildlife agencies have traditionally undervalued black bears. Until 1989, for example, BC allowed hunters to kill up to five black bears a year. Hunters are still allowed

Black bears eat insects that colonize dead trees and logs.

two in many parts of the West. Farmers and ranchers are not legally required to store forage or animal carcasses in bear-proof containers, leading to chronic "bear problems." When wildlife officers are called in because of black bears attracted to poorly stored garbage, they frequently don't even bother to relocate the bear. They kill it. Thus irresponsible human behaviour turns into a bear problem and is solved at the expense of the bear.

One small wooden granary building just north of Waterton Lakes National Park became notorious as a black hole for bears. The rancher found it easier and cheaper to phone for a conservation officer than to bear-proof his oat storage shed. Many dozens of black bears died before the rancher finally replaced his leaky building with a bear-proof metal granary, and that only happened because a conservation group agreed to pay for the new structure. Fortunately for the area's bear population, his neighbours were more progressive.

The risks inherent in a style of bear management that relies too heavily on simply killing "problem bears" became apparent in a 1980s study in Banff National Park. For most of the twentieth century, Banff, like most national parks, managed its garbage and sloppy campers by shooting bears. That began to change in the 1980s, when park officials decided to invest in some basic population research to learn more about the bears – the first time the most intensively managed animal in the western national parks had ever been studied!

The findings were a shock to park managers, who had always assumed they had, if anything, too many black bears. In fact, there were fewer than twenty black bears in the Bow River valley. The unrestrained killing of bears by park authorities – combined with half a century of gradual habitat loss because of fire suppression and tourism development – was beginning to threaten the very existence of black bears in Canada's oldest national park.

In places like the Rocky Mountain national parks, where campgrounds and resorts are scattered throughout the best bear habitats, black bears can seem more common than they really are. Unless campers are consistently responsible and resort operators are conscientious in dealing with garbage and other waste, bears continue to be drawn into the developed areas well after their numbers have dropped perilously low. People who estimate bear populations from the number of bear problems or the frequency of sightings in developed areas are actually just dealing with an index of human sloppiness. Sightings are almost meaningless in estimating bear numbers.

By the same token, hunters and outfitters who use bait stations to attract bears often remain convinced that black bears are abundant well after hunting kills exceed the ability of the local bear population to replace the losses. If there's a bear left in the area, chances are good it will visit a bait station – so, to the hunter in the blind, there is no sign of bear scarcity.

Shooting bears over bait, of course, is not true hunting. It can have a devastating effect on bear populations, both by causing too many to die and by training the survivors to associate humans with food. It is, however, regulated by wildlife authorities. Poachers, who sometimes use bait too, are a bigger threat because their activities are driven by greed and entirely unregulated.

Protecting black bears

Measures bear biologists agree would help ensure a future for the black bear:

- ban the use of bait and hounds in bear hunting
- make possession or sale of gallbladders, bear paws or other body parts illegal once they have been removed from a carcass
- physically close logging roads, mining exploration roads and seismic cutlines and prohibit their use by off-road vehicles
- protect prime bear habitats from human development
- close or bear-proof local garbage dumps and prevent access by bears to garbage, human food and domestic livestock

Poaching prospectus

Estimated illegal kills of bears in North America each year	100,000
Cash price for a poached gallbladder in Canada	$125–$225
Cash price for a poached gallbladder in Asia	$1,250–$2,250
Processed value of a gallbladder in the Asian marketplace	$50,000
Number of bowls of soup made from one bear paw	6
Price for a bowl of bear paw soup	$250

GALLBLADDERS, CLAWS AND CRIME

The Humane Society of Canada estimates that legal hunting accounts for less than half of the actual human-caused black bear mortality. Poachers – some of whom masquerade as legal hunters and bear outfitters – may be killing more than forty thousand Canadian black bears every year to sell gallbladders, claws and other parts of bears into a lucrative illegal market. Poaching has become a multi-million dollar business in recent decades, due to lucrative markets for bear gallbladders and other body parts in China and other Asian countries. As trade relationships between Canada and eastern Asia continue to improve, creating more potential pipelines for the illicit movement of bear parts, the problem will likely grow.

A Canadian Wildlife Federation report states that "the illegal traffic in wildlife has been likened to that in drugs, each being capable of yielding high profits. However, the small penalties typically meted out to people convicted of poaching and illegal animal trade make those activities much safer than drug dealing…"

Gallbladders sell in North America for more than twenty dollars per gram, making them worth more than many illegal drugs. In fact, they are drugs: bear gallbladders are ground up to yield ursodeoxycholic acid, producing such traditional Chinese medicines as *Fel Ursi,* which is used to treat a wide variety of ailments. By the time a bear gallbladder actually makes it into the Asian marketplace it may be worth as much as $50,000 – almost twenty times the price of its weight in gold. Meanwhile, claws and feet are used to make soup and ornaments believed to enhance the power of those who use them.

The market in bear body parts has led to the rapid decimation of bear populations in Asia and other parts of the world. The worst offenders are South Korea, Hong Kong (the main conduit through which illegal gallbladders are shipped), Taiwan, Japan and China. In some parts of China, large numbers of bears are held in tiny pens with steel tubing inserted into their gallbladders. The bears are "milked" for gall, an excruciatingly cruel process. It generates great wealth for the practitioners, but the bears survive this torment for less than ten years, dying of infections and other causes at only a third the normal life expectancy of wild bears.

Proponents of bear farming argue that one captive bear can produce enough gall in its lifetime to save the lives of 220 wild bears that might otherwise be poached.

"It's horrendous what the Chinese government is doing, what they're encouraging," counters Charlie Russell. "They have ten thousand of these farmed bears, and they want forty thousand. They encourage taking them out of the wild to stock the bear farms. The health of the animals is horrendous. It's just a sad scene."

Internationally, illegal profits from bear poaching exceed $6-million a year, according to the Humane Society. A 1995 investigation by Environment Canada, the RCMP and BC's Ministry of Environment turned up 191 bear galls and 84 bear paws in several Chinese businesses in Vancouver. Investigators know that, as with most organized crime, they are barely scratching the surface.

Steve Peterson of the Alaska Department of Fish and Game feels that the problem tends to be overstated by wildlife officers. "Some of those guys say that the problem's so bad we're going to run out of bears in five years," he says, "and that's just not true. If there were lots of bears being poached for their gallbladders, we'd be finding carcasses out in the woods with just their bellies ripped open, and we're not. Too many enforcement guys see a crook behind every bush."

In some accessible areas, however, bears are in fact being found with their bellies ripped open. A popular Riding Mountain National Park black bear was found in this condition at an isolated garbage dump. His gallbladder and paws were missing, and the rest of his carcass had been left to rot.

The illegal activity is made easier by the proliferation of logging and other roads that provide poachers access to remote areas, the recent legalization of setting bait for bears, and government cutbacks that have reduced the ability of wildlife agencies to conduct undercover investigations. Possession of gallbladders is still legal in most states and provinces, which makes it hard for wildlife investigators to secure convictions for trafficking. Worse, according to biologist Wayne McCrory, the government of the Northwest Territories still allows the legal marketing of bear body parts.

Monte Hummel and Sherry Pettigrew, authors of the World Wildlife Fund Canada book *Wild Hunters*, say the illegal trade in bear body parts "has already seriously endangered several Asian bear species, leading to concern about whether North American bears aren't far behind."

Charlie Russell agrees: "The problem of gallbladders is definitely the most serious for bears worldwide. I don't know what we can do. Talking to the Chinese, it's not just a medicine. It's a status symbol. Emperors were the only ones that were able to afford this medicine, but now there's a lot of people that can afford it in China. They want it as a status symbol. It's like driving a Mercedes."

Setting bait for bears

Real hunters normally hunt black bears by stalking ones they've spotted from a distance with binoculars. They glass open slopes, tangles of berry bushes and other likely feeding areas or, less commonly, still-hunt slowly along game trails in good bear habitat. It isn't easy. Well more than half the hopeful bear hunters go home empty-handed at season's end. Even so, this kind of experience strengthens their bond to nature and leaves them with enriching memories.

Over the past quarter century, however, a new, more surefire technique of collecting a bear rug has gained acceptance across most of western Canada. Baiting virtually assures a kill, while eliminating the need for skill or woodcraft.

Baiting is particularly popular with commercial outfitters, allowing them to offer their clients guaranteed kills. Wildlife investigators have found that some outfitters add to their profits by illegally selling gallbladders from the bears their hunters take over bait stations.

Baiting takes advantage of the inability of most bears to resist easy pickings. The so-called "hunters" set out barrels of food in remote forested areas a week or two before the hunting season. Baiting seasons correspond with periods when black bears are most urgently seeking food: early spring and late fall. Consequently, by the time hunting season opens, most of the bears in the area will be visiting the bait station.

Biologist Paul Paquet watched sixteen different black bears visit one bait station near Riding Mountain National Park over the course of one four-hour period. He found that nearly all the bears that live in the 2,970-square-kilometre park are susceptible to hunters' bait stations just outside park boundaries. He also noted that when female black bears approach bait stations, they usually leave their cubs behind until they have checked the barrels out. Hunters are not legally allowed to shoot mothers with cubs. Even so, many are not aware of this behaviour and kill nursing mothers unintentionally.

When Teddy Roosevelt, George Bird Grinnell and other American sportsmen founded the Boone & Crockett Club in 1887 and established a trophy system for scoring big game, they hoped to eliminate unethical hunting behaviour. One of their explicit principles was that hunting must involve "fair chase." They argued that sportsmanlike restraint and the practice of woods skills made not only better hunters but better people.

The legalization of setting bait for bears – which involves no chase at all – strikes many hunters as a serious lowering of ethical standards. It unfairly exploits black bears' inability to resist readily accessible and energy-rich food. Fair chase doesn't even come into the picture. Nor does hunting skill.

Baiting is not hunting – it's simply an easy way to kill bears.

And it kills a lot of them.

What's legal?

Province/State	Hunting	Baiting	Hunting with hounds	Possession of gallbladders	Sale of gallbladders
Manitoba	Yes	Yes	No	No	No
Saskatche-wan	Yes	Yes	No	Yes	No
Alberta	Yes	Yes	No	Yes	No
BC	Yes	No	Yes	No	No
NWT	Yes	Yes	Yes	Yes	Yes
Yukon	Yes	No	No	Yes	No
Alaska	Yes	Yes	Yes	Yes	No
Oregon	Yes	No	No	Yes	No
Washington	Yes	No	No	Yes	No
Idaho	Yes	Yes	Yes	Yes	Yes
Montana	Yes	No	No	Yes	No
Wyoming	Yes	Yes	No	Yes	No

BLACK BEAR HUNTING

The World Wildlife Fund says that hunting threatens some local black bear populations, especially where bait-setting is legal and backwoods roads remain open

Because they wander more widely than females, male black bears are more often killed by hunters.

162

for public use. Wayne McCrory says some wildlife agencies regularly allow hunters to kill more bears than the population can spare. He also suspects that up to 25 per cent of the bears shot by hunters don't even turn up in official statistics, because they escape, wounded, to die later.

Hunting hasn't historically posed a threat to black bear populations. Some provincial game biologists, in fact, argue that hunting can even increase bear numbers. Hunters kill more males than females: males wander more widely, are less wary and make the largest trophies. Some mature male black bears kill young bears, so game biologists believe that moderate hunting can allow more young bears to survive until maturity. A study near Cold Lake, Alberta, supported this premise: when researchers killed dominant male bears, the bear population doubled.

Some wildlife managers believe hunting teaches black bears to become more timid and less likely to become problems around farms and towns. No scientific evidence supports this theory, and as more than one biologist has wryly pointed out, dead bears don't learn. Charlie Russell is among others who feel that bears taught to fear humans are actually more dangerous than those that trust us.

Either way, there is no question that hunting can become a problem where hunters gain unfair advantages.

Tim Thier studied black bears in the Yahk River watershed of southeastern BC. Hunters killed ten of his twenty-two radio-collared study bears within a single year. The many logging roads that criss-crossed his research area ensured great access for hunters. Numerous clear-cuts meant that bears had difficulty staying out of sight.

Closing unnecessary roads so that hunters have to walk may do far more to protect bear populations than restrictive hunting regulations. Unfortunately, most government wildlife agencies have little say about road closures – the final decisions rest with land use agencies which base their rulings not on wildlife needs but on government resource development policies. Forest companies, oil and gas companies and off-road-vehicle lobby groups often have as much influence over road access decisions as biologists do, if not more.

Wildlife managers try to mitigate the impact of uncontrolled road access by making hunting seasons shorter or limiting the number of hunters. But this has no effect on the more serious problem of poaching. Some experts estimate that poachers kill two bears for every one shot legally by a hunter. Open roads and off-road vehicle trails are like self-serve bear dispensers for criminals, especially when government cutbacks mean fewer wildlife officers in the field.

STAYING SAFE IN BLACK BEAR COUNTRY

Black bears appear harmless and inoffensive as they graze on dandelions and clover along the edges of national park highways. Usually they are.

But every harmless-looking black bear is potentially dangerous. In some ways, the seemingly benign nature of black bears leads humans to take more chances around them than around their much-feared relative, the grizzly. In reality, however, black bears have killed

A black bear stressed by humans approaching too close can become dangerous.

four times as many people as grizzlies in BC, and they account for more than 80 per cent of all human injuries and property damage by bears in North America.

Bears that have learned to associate humans with food can become dangerous; they are also doomed. That's why national park staff confiscate coolers, barbecues and other smelly items from unattended campsites – the most unpleasant part of a park ranger's job involves killing a bear that human irresponsibility has spoiled.

Black bears that normally tolerate or ignore nearby people can become aggressive when they start to feel

A black bear can run twice as fast as a human.

crowded or harassed. Usually the aggression takes the form of a warning stomp of the front feet, or the bear turns sideways to make its body appear larger. Most black bears would rather bluff than fight. Only very rarely, usually because it feels threatened by having its retreat cut off or being approached too closely, does a black bear attack.

Even a bluff charge can be dangerous, as one tourist discovered on Banff's Icefields Parkway. Trying to get a good photograph, the man moved too close to a black bear which suddenly stopped foraging and bluff-charged him. He jumped back, and a passing car struck and killed him.

Roadside bears can be irresistible attractions, but as the size of the human crowd increases, the collective intelligence level seems to decrease. People in a crowd do things they would never dream of doing alone. Bear jams produce incredibly bizarre human behaviour – fathers holding their children close to wild bears for photographs, photographers circling behind bears, people even holding out their hands to be sniffed, as if bears were pet dogs.

Surprisingly few serious attacks occur at bear jams. Black bears are remarkably tolerant of stupidity.

Very rarely, black bears prey on people. Between 1900 and 2009, black bears killed a total of sixty-three people in fifty-nine different attacks across North America. Stephen Herrero and researcher Andrew Higgins reviewed the circumstances of each attack and concluded that 88 per cent of the attacks were predatory, mostly involving adult male black bears. Most of the attacks occurred after 1960, and most were in Canada and Alaska.

Herrero and Higgins speculated that the reason Canada and Alaska have seen more predatory attacks than the lower forty-eight United States is because northern bears often live in marginal habitats. Hunger can make them more desperate than bears living in more productive environments.

Small children, solitary hikers and anglers who remain still for long periods are most at risk from these rare attacks. Given that, it's good practice to hike or camp in groups, remain alert at all times and supervise children closely. Consider any bear that openly approaches, deliberately stalks or tries to circle behind you as a dangerous animal. It wants something it shouldn't.

The prudent solution when confronted by a bold black bear is to retreat inside a vehicle or building. Yelling, holding up your arms or otherwise making yourself appear dangerous may out-bluff the animal if retreat isn't an option. Distracting it with something edible may also buy you time to escape, but rewarding the bear will probably encourage it to be even more aggressive next time.

Playing dead for a predatory bear is a bad idea – you're just saving it some work. If a bear you believe to be a black bear attacks in circumstances where it is clearly being the aggressor, fight back aggressively and loudly.

But it shouldn't ever come to that if you are alert and carrying a can of bear spray. Anyone spending a lot of time in black bear habitat should carry capsicum-based bear spray. It is an extremely effective last-resort defence. Keep a can readily accessible on a belt, a pack strap or a fishing vest at all times. Research has shown that pepper spray is more effective against an attacking bear than a gun.

Prevention, the best cure
Prevention is the key to staying safe in black bear country:
- show bears the respect they deserve: watch from a distance, move slowly, and leave if human activity causes the bear to stop feeding or become more watchful

- keep all food, garbage or other items that might attract bears safely locked away, especially at night
- pay attention to your surroundings, and carry bear spray

Keep your pants on!

Park wardens expect to see a lot of unusual sights while on patrol, but Darro Stinson never expected to turn a corner on Jasper's Icefields Parkway and find two naked people huddled forlornly beside a locked car. The black bear studying them from the highway shoulder looked more curious than hungry, but the couple obviously had more goose bumps from fear than from the cool mountain air.

Stinson made room for them in the front seat of his truck and offered his jacket to the young lady, who seemed particularly upset by the whole situation.

Then he opened his notebook and took down the details with all the professional detachment he could muster, under the circumstances.

It seems the young couple, overcome with the romantic ambience of the Rockies and the warmth of their feelings for one another, had decided to head off into the woods to find a quiet place where they could commune with nature. They soon became so engrossed that they forgot all about nature – until a loud snort told the duo that they were now a trio.

In the haste of their departure for the safety of their car, neither realized that the car keys were still in the pocket of a pair of pants left behind – along with the rest of their clothes – in the woods.

The bear, no doubt fascinated by the behaviour of these strange creatures, decided to stay and see what they would do next. Luckily, especially given all the mosquitoes, a park warden was on duty that day.

The moral of this story: keep your pants on in bear country. If you can't do that, then at least keep the car keys in your hand.

6

GRIZZLY BEAR

Ursus arctos horribilis

Strange though it may seem, the dancing bears of medieval circuses and the chained bears that once fought dogs to the death for the entertainment of English nobility were the same species as North America's silvertip grizzlies and Kodiak bears. The grizzly, in fact, is one continental subpopulation of the most widely distributed species of bear in the world. *Ursus arctos*, the brown bear, ranges from the Pyrenees and Alps of Europe all across Asia, through parts of China and Japan, to Siberia, Alaska and down the western half of North America to Wyoming.

The famous Kodiak bear, which can grow as large as 600 kilograms (1,300 pounds), is found on Kodiak, Afognak and Shuyak Islands. It may be descended, with other coastal Alaska grizzlies, from ancestors that found their way from Asia into the lush tidal flats and rainforests of North America's farthest shores forty thousand years ago. They were among many Asian species that colonized Beringia – a broad plain that joined eastern Siberia to coastal Alaska during the Pleistocene ice age. Taxonomists believe the rest of the North American grizzlies are descended from brown bears that spread south only about fifteen thousand years ago, when the great glaciers melted.

Grizzly bear facts

Length	1.8–2.5 m (5.5–7.5 ft.)
Weight	130–400 kg (280–900 lb.); Kodiaks grow larger
Description	Brown, ranging from almost blonde to almost black; often with a grizzled appearance on the back, shoulders and head. Pronounced hump at front shoulders, long claws on forepaws, and a dish-shaped face with small ears.
Reproduction	First breeds at 5–7 years; has 1–3 cubs every three or more years
Lifespan	30 years
Diet	Plants, insects, meat
Distribution	Northern US Rockies, extreme western Alberta, most of BC, and from Alaska east to Hudson Bay

"... a Bear which is Bigger than any white Bear and is Neither White nor Black, But silver-hair'd like our English Rabbit...."

—Henry Kelsey, 1691, first European
to describe the grizzly

Japan's grizzlies

More *Ursus arctos* now live in the wild on one island in Japan – the 77,000-square-kilometre Hokkaido – than in the continental US. An estimated three thousand bears thrive in its forested coastal areas. Hokkaido's bear habitats are lush and productive, so bears need much smaller home ranges than their North American relatives do. The high density of both bears and people, unfortunately, leads to frequent conflicts. Originally held in high esteem by the native Ainu people, in whose language the bear is *kimun-kamui*, or "the god that lives in mountains," bears are now frequently killed to protect agricultural crops or are illegally poached to supply the gallbladder trade.

Ursus arctos once ranged even more widely than it does today. Brown bears lived in Ireland until about 750 CE and survived in Great Britain for two or three centuries more. They lingered in the dark forests of Germany until the late 1700s and were eradicated from the Swiss and French Alps early in the twentieth century.

By that time, North American populations were shrinking too. The grizzlies that once ranged down the river valleys of the Great Plains and south along the Mississippi were virtually extinct by the beginning of the twentieth century. California may at one time have been the centre of North American abundance for the great bears, with an estimated population of ten thousand grizzlies, but the last survivors were finally killed in the early 1920s, leaving the Golden Bear State without any golden bears.

From Mexico north, European settlement of the American West filled the valleys with livestock, farms, towns and railroads. Excluded from the valleys, grizzly populations were fragmented and isolated on island-like mountain ranges where whites and natives alike hunted them mercilessly for the fur trade. When some learned to kill domestic sheep and cattle, the invading ranchers used repeating rifles, metal leg-hold traps, hounds and poisons in a ruthless war of extermination. One by one, as these "island" populations dwindled below the point where they could recover, grizzly populations winked out.

Arizona's last grizzly was killed in 1935. The last known Mexico grizzly was shot in 1965, although a few optimistic biologists persist in the hope that a small population may survive in the Sierra Madre. Colorado's last grizzly was killed in 1979, a quarter century after most experts thought the bear had been extirpated from that state. New Mexico, Utah, Nevada, Oregon … most western states are now haunted only by the ghosts of grizzlies that used to be.

The extinction process continues today, with island populations of grizzlies hanging on in the Greater Yellowstone Ecosystem, where Montana, Idaho and Wyoming abut one another, and in three other isolated mountain ranges in northern Montana. Biologists estimate that half of Canada's grizzlies survive today in British Columbia, but even there, hydroelectric reservoirs, towns and agricultural development isolate many grizzly subpopulations that face a growing risk of dying out one by one.

In an exhaustive 1990 review of the grizzly bear's status, the Committee on the Status of Endangered

Wildlife in Canada concluded that more than 60 per cent of grizzly habitat is threatened by human activities. Although the federal government has so far chosen not to classify the grizzly under Canada's Species at Risk Act, the bear is blue-listed under BC legislation (meaning it is vulnerable and could become threatened or endangered). The Province of Alberta recognizes the grizzly as a threatened species.

The plains grizzly

David Thompson, the great early nineteenth-century map-maker and explorer, encountered grizzly bears when he reached the Saskatchewan River, well out on the prairies, and throughout his explorations of western Canada.

Fifty years later, the Palliser expedition ran into grizzly bears along the lower Red Deer River and near modern-day Medicine Hat, well east of where they occur today.

John "Kootenai" Brown, an adventurer who later became the first park warden in Waterton Lakes National Park, wrote that when he first arrived in the region in 1865 "... there roamed all along the south branch of the Saskatchewan River hundreds of grizzly bear, small grizzlies, but grizzlies just the same."

The world of the plains grizzly was one of abundance: millions of bison, countless elk and antelope, thickets of berry-producing shrubs, roots and lush vegetation along wild prairie rivers. The great bears probably spent most of their time in the cottonwood forests and shrubbery along rivers, streams and coulees and in isolated hill systems like the Cypress, Sweet Grass and Neutral

Hills. They ranged as far east as Manitoba, even into parts of Ontario, and south as far as western Oklahoma and Texas. In the eastern portion of their range, grizzlies were able to feed on oak mast, wild grapes and other seasonal foods not available farther west.

The original people of the Great Plains respected and feared the grizzly. Until traders arrived with metal arrowheads, and later with firearms, First Peoples had no effective protection against the great bears.

The hunting and gathering lives of the Siksika, Piikani, Kainai and other tribes put them in frequent danger from the plains grizzly. These tribes relied heavily on the plains bison for food. They often chased large numbers of bison off cliffs, into traps known as buffalo pounds or into deep snow drifts. There they slaughtered all they could and camped near the carcasses until they had finished stripping them of meat, hides and other products.

Grizzlies, able to detect the smell of dead bison from great distances, must have gravitated to these kill sites. Many early explorers' journals describe grizzlies scavenging on bison remains along prairie rivers.

First Nations people also relied heavily on saskatoons, chokecherries and other berries. This often put the women who gathered them into close contact with grizzly bears that relied on the same seasonal food source.

Artist Paul Kane, camped among the Cree near Fort Edmonton in 1845, wrote that "there is no animal on the whole continent that the Indians hold in so much dread as the grisly [sic] bear, and few will attack one of them alone, unless with a very fleet horse under him..."

The repeating rifle and strychnine, both of which arrived in western Canada in the early 1870s, brought the reign of the great bear to a sudden end. One trading post in the Cypress Hills area took in 750 "grizzle" hides in a single year. By the late 1800s, commercial hunting had eradicated grizzlies from the plains.

A few grizzlies managed to survive through the twentieth century in what once was part of the range of the plains grizzly – Montana's Pine Butte Swamp Preserve and Blackfeet Indian Reservation, and along the eastern edge of the Waterton–Glacier International Peace Park. They live year-round in valley-floor willow thickets and the intermingled bunchgrass prairie and aspen bluffs that spill east from the Rocky Mountains.

These populations began to expand eastward in the twenty-first century. Pheasant hunters now frequently encounter grizzlies along the Teton River, well east of the Rockies. In Alberta, a mother and her cubs spent several months in the prairie coulees near Whiskey Gap. One young male, captured near Loma, Montana, after killing a domestic sheep, had wandered almost to the Missouri River breaks where Lewis and Clark encountered the original prairie bears.

The plains grizzly may soon be back.

Death cry

"A few days after our arrival, the death cry was given ... The cry was from a young man who held his bow and arrows and showed one of his thighs torn by a grizzled bear ... which had killed two of his companions. The old man called for his powder horn and shot bag, and, seeing the priming of his gun in good order, he set off with the young man for the bear, which was at a short distance. They found him devouring one of the dead. The moment he saw them he sat up on his hind legs, showing them his teeth and long clawed paws. In this, his usual position to defend his prey, his head is a bad mark, but his breast offers a direct mark to the heart, through which the old man sent his ball and killed him.

"The two young men who were destroyed by the bear had each two iron-shod arrows, and, the camp being near, they attacked him for his skin and claws, but unfortunately their arrows stuck in the bones of his ribs, and only irritated him...

"The first poor fellow was still alive, and knew his parents, in whose arms he expired. The bear, for the mischief he had done, was condemned to be burnt to ashes. The claws of his forepaws, very sharp and long, the young man wanted for a collar but it was not granted; those that burned the bear watched until nothing but ashes remained."

—David Thompson, 1787, near the present site of Calgary

HABITAT

The grizzly is a creature of the whole landscape. It doesn't have just one habitat; it has many. Its most important habitats are where fire, flood or avalanches have opened up the vegetation cover. Burned forests, with their abundant berries, rotting logs full of ants, and edible plants like sweetvetch and blueberries are particular favourites. A landscape where dams have tamed the rivers, or where natural fire has been eliminated, is a landscape that no longer looks quite so much like home to a grizzly bear.

Along the west coast, grizzlies forage in old-growth temperate rainforest where small-scale disturbances like wind-thrown trees create small openings full of greenery. In the interior mountains and plateaus, they prefer burned areas or wander along flood-scarred river flats where they fish for spawning salmon or trout in season, dig roots or graze on succulent plants like tufted hairgrass. They venture up meltwater gullies to eat young horsetail foliage, then wander out onto avalanche slopes, where they find abundant green vegetation, berries and, in spring, sometimes an avalanche-killed elk or mountain goat.

Some human activities create habitats that resemble natural ones. Logging, for example, removes the tree canopy just as fire does. Logged areas – until replanted trees grow large enough to shade the soil – can be rich sources of huckleberries and other sustenance. Unlike fire, however, logging removes the large tree trunks that would otherwise fall over and become habitat for ants and other bear foods. It leaves few patches of standing live trees to provide shelter. In addition, logging disturbs the soil, killing the roots of important bear food plants and opening up the forest floor to invasion by weeds such as Canada thistle. Government regulations, in fact, require many logging companies to scarify (plough) the soil when they are finished cutting, to create seed beds for new conifer trees. Worse, some logging companies use herbicides to kill plants they feel compete with commercial tree species, even though bears depend on some of these plants. A second-growth forest after logging is an impoverished ecosystem compared to one resulting from wildfire or natural bark beetle outbreaks.

Logging roads pose more problems. When the loggers go home, their roads usually remain open to hunters, berry pickers and mountain bikers. Studies have shown that when road densities exceed 0.6 kilometres for every square kilometre of landscape, as they do in many logged watersheds, grizzly death rates from legal and illegal killing increase. Even though the population density decreases with each dead bear, the survivors continue to gravitate to the good feeding habitat along roads, where their high visibility sustains the illusion that there are still plenty of bears.

Ski hills create artificial habitat similar in some ways to avalanche slopes. But ski hills rarely achieve their potential for grizzly bears. Most ski hill operators encourage people to hike and bike the runs during summer, and many people either don't know how to coexist with bears or don't want to. The Lake Louise Ski Area, in Banff National Park, is a notable exception. There, grizzly families often feed on the moist, grassy slopes while tourists are able to enjoy them from the electric-fenced base area or from a gondola passing overhead.

Floods, fires, avalanches and low human use translate into high-quality grizzly habitat. Roads, garbage and high human use usually mean poor grizzly habitat. For the most part, grizzlies continue to thrive only in areas where humans have chosen to protect natural landscapes in large parks and wilderness areas or to limit the number of roads and developments. Some land management agencies have begun closing and reclaiming roads in some forest areas, improving the odds that the West's wounded watersheds may again become good places for grizzlies.

Barely surviving

The most secure grizzly populations in the western United States survive in the Rocky Mountains – in and around Glacier and Yellowstone National Parks. Elsewhere, isolated populations hover on the very brink of extinction.

Fewer than forty grizzlies survive in the North Cascades, which straddle the international boundary between Washington and BC. Farther east, about sixty grizzlies range the Selkirk Mountains on both sides of the international border.

Along with another forty grizzlies occupying the Cabinet Mountains farther south, these dangerously small populations are the last that survive south of the 49th parallel outside the Rockies. Other, similarly small populations once survived farther south but, one by one, they winked out and were gone forever.

Small, isolated populations are at risk from habitat loss, inbreeding or simple bad luck. In 2009 the last five caribou in Banff National Park died in an avalanche. Similar calamities – perhaps a particularly intense and widespread forest fire – could wipe out a small grizzly population.

Governmental and private organizations are working to secure the future for these isolated bear populations, mostly by protecting productive habitat and reducing human activity in their core ranges.

In 2008 the Nature Conservancy of Canada acquired the six hundred square kilometre Darkwoods Conservation Area in the Canadian part of the Selkirk Mountains. On the US side, the Vital Ground Foundation has led the way in securing private land with high habitat values. In the longer term, the best hope for isolated bear populations is land use planning that reconnects their habitat with that of other bears.

Mile-high grizzlies

Most people believed that Colorado's last grizzly bear died in 1952. In 1979, however, a bowhunter and his guide, Ed Wiseman, blundered into a bear high in the San Juan Mountains. Fleeing from the hunter, the panicked bear attacked Wiseman. He managed to snatch up a fallen arrow and stab the bear twice. The second wound penetrated to the bear's heart. The old grizzly turned away, lay down against a log, rested her muzzle on her paw, and died.

The discovery of a grizzly more than a quarter century after the species had been declared extirpated created quite a stir – especially when a post-mortem revealed that the old bear had nursed young during her lifetime.

State biologists searched but found no more evidence of grizzlies. Rather than accept the official "maybe," conservation activist Doug Peacock launched the San Juan Grizzly Project in 1992. Each summer, teams of students hiked into the high country in search of tracks, scat, diggings or – even better – grizzly sightings. The researchers turned up some promising evidence, but definitive proof eluded them. Nobody knows whether a few last grizzlies survive in southwestern Colorado.

A growing number of Coloradans, however, believe they probably ought to know. The San Juans contain some of the most productive grizzly bear habitat in the American West, and ample space for the great bears to roam.

And sightings keep dribbling in. As recently as 2006, hunters reported seeing a mother grizzly with two cubs in the San Isabel National Forest, near Aspen and well outside the San Juan Mountains. The sighting was considered credible enough to trigger a search by Division of Wildlife staff, but they found no further evidence of the bears. If these were indeed grizzlies, then it is more likely that they found their way there from the expanding Greater Yellowstone Ecosystem population in Wyoming than that they were part of a surviving Colorado population.

That might be the best-case option, according to David Petersen, who helped investigate rumours of a few surviving grizzlies in Colorado. In his book *Ghost Grizzlies*, he describes the history of grizzlies in the San Juans and the ambivalence many conservationists feel about grizzly bear recovery. If any grizzlies survive, he says, it might be best to simply to leave them alone. Importing grizzlies from Yellowstone or Canada, as some groups promote, would likely only result in dead bears and political conflict that could hasten the demise of any last local survivors.

Even so, Petersen shares a sentiment that has become increasingly prevalent in Colorado: "We should work to save the grizzly, because it is power, passion and freedom embodied. It is our own worst nightmare and our most beautiful dream. It is wildness personified."

FAMILY LIFE

Female grizzlies can be fiercely protective mothers. They need to be.

A female grizzly will usually be five or more years old before she is ready to breed and then, if all goes well, she will produce only two or three cubs every three years. Ecologically, grizzly bears compensate for such a low reproduction rate – the lowest of any North American mammal – by being attentive mothers, extremely aggressive in defence of their offspring.

A grizzly mother nursing her cubs.

After mating in June, a female grizzly goes about her life as if nothing much has happened, which in a way is true. The fertilized egg doesn't attach itself to her uterine wall and start to grow until after she enters her den late in the fall. Pregnancy is on hold until she has fattened up and found a safe place to give birth.

The tiny, blind cubs – about the size of a shoe – are born in mid-winter while their mother hibernates. For the first few months, their life is a confined and comfortable one of nursing, warmth and nurture inside their birth den. In April they emerge blinking into their first high-country spring. This is the beginning of an intensive education into the nature of the landscape in which they will have to survive, and it is also the beginning of the most dangerous part of their lives. Mortality is far higher among young grizzlies than among fully grown adults. Most cub mortality happens during the first year of life.

The cubs spend two or three years with their mother, denning with her each winter and following her around her home range. This extended childhood ensures that their mother can teach them to find and recognize their various seasonal foods, and that she can protect them until they have grown to nearly adult size. Cubs are vulnerable to large predators like wolves and cougars, but the greatest danger facing them may well be their father – some male grizzlies have been known to kill or harass cubs and young bears. Female grizzlies often choose to raise their cubs in marginal habitat seldom visited by males, in order to reduce the risk of a confrontation. If this strategy fails, however, a female can be desperately fierce in defence of her cubs.

Cubs play with one another and their mother a great deal, clearly demonstrating both affection and enjoyment during periods when they aren't travelling or feeding. The bond between sibling cubs may survive for months or even years after they leave their mother, even after the cubs have adopted the more solitary lifestyle typical of an adult grizzly.

The Cairn Pass orphans

Park warden Norm Woodie spotted the female grizzly too late as he rode into an open timberline meadow. Trailed by her three cubs, she loped toward him. Woodie thought she was just curious, but when she had got too close to make a comfortable retreat, she decided her cubs were at risk. She suddenly laid back her ears and broke into a full-fledged charge.

Woodie's warning shots had no effect. At last, with the bear only a few metres away, he shot her in self-defence. In 1975, bear spray wasn't an option.

Park wardens always find the death of a female grizzly hard to stomach, but this one was particularly galling. Woodie was part of a joint Parks Canada/Canadian Wildlife Service study intended to help grizzlies stay alive.

Woodie and his research colleagues faced a further dilemma: the dead mother had left behind three orphaned cubs barely six months old. Nobody had ever heard of grizzlies that small surviving in the wild.

After discussing the options, the team decided to leave the cubs alone and hope for the best. They ended that field season with heavy hearts, worried that the incident may have caused the deaths of four bears.

When the researchers returned to their study area the following May, however, they found all three cubs digging sweetvetch roots on a timberline knoll near Cairn Pass. The bears' small size showed they had endured a stressful first year of life, but at least they were alive. The bears spent the whole summer in or near Cairn Pass, feeding mostly on sweetvetch roots, although on one occasion they stole a marmot from a coyote and spent almost an hour chasing and being chased by their victim. The cubs were inseparable, playing for hours and often hugging one another.

In late August one cub disappeared, probably killed by a large male grizzly in the area. The survivors appeared nervous and uneasy at first, but within a few days they had recovered their spirits and played and dug roots as if nothing had changed.

Next spring, the cubs were still alive, although noticeably smaller than other grizzlies their age. Tracks in the snow showed they had spent the winter in the den where they had been born

The cubs ultimately spent four years together before separating in 1979. By then the researchers had gained valuable insights into the life of grizzly bear cubs and the impact of losing their mother early. The orphans remained attached to one another longer than usual. They were undersized, wary of humans, vulnerable to predation and reluctant to leave the area they had explored with their mother. In late summer, when other bears were eating berries, the cubs ate only the sweet-vetch roots, grass and other early season plants their mother had showed them before her death.

SOCIAL LIFE

Conventional wisdom is that grizzlies don't have much of a social life. Most sightings of grizzlies involve single bears. The only time a grizzly appears interested in spending much time in the company of another is during the mating season. Even that seems a transient affair at best, with both animals parting ways soon after mating. Males will travel great distances in late spring, searching for breeding-age females. If they find a female with cubs, they may try to isolate the female from her offspring – it's often during the mating season that females separate from their young. I once watched a female with two yearling cubs spend most of a week clambering around on cliffs that would challenge a mountain goat, peering down into the timber, where a large male lurked hopefully.

Grizzlies live mostly solitary lives.

Once a dominant male finds a female in heat, he shadows her constantly. As she reaches the receptive stage of her breeding cycle, the male will herd her into some other isolated area and hold her there until finally she is ready to mate. In the Rockies, male grizzlies sometimes corral a female on a mountain ridge, chasing her and heading her off when she tries to escape down into the trees. Grizzlies mate repeatedly over a period of days before the two animals suddenly lose interest in each other. There may be another brief mating period a few weeks later, but by the end of June the bears are alone again.

Younger male bears have a different mating strategy than the more dominant older males: they cruise constantly in hopes of a brief fling, but move on quickly rather than try to defend a mate against stronger males.

Males wander much more widely than females, marking their home ranges not only with their droppings and urine but by clawing or rubbing against marker trees. Such trees can be recognized by claw marks, tufts of hair stuck in the bark, and smooth surfaces from repeated rubbing. Some of these trees have clearly defined trails approaching them, where bears place their paws in exactly the same position each time they visit the tree. Biologist Cam McTavish has studied photo sequences from motion-triggered cameras trained on these bear trees. He says the bears adopt a deliberate, twisting movement of their forelegs as they draw near, almost a ritualistic march, which biologists have yet to understand.

When bears meet, they quickly establish dominance by posturing, bluff charging or threatening one another, and the underdog soon takes to his heels. If he doesn't, a fight may result, with both bears roaring and gripping one another, biting at each other's jaws and head until one surrenders, is wounded or suffers mortal injuries.

Large home ranges and intolerance for other bears are among the main reasons why grizzly bears are relatively scarce even at the best of times; there just isn't enough room in the landscape for a lot of grizzlies.

But the intolerance of grizzlies for one another breaks down when food is abundant, suggesting that the real factor that keeps bears sparsely distributed and solitary is the need to parcel out limited food supplies. Along some coastal salmon streams, large numbers of grizzly bears can sometimes be seen sharing the rich harvest of spawning fish. At Alaska's McNeil River

Falls, visitors can see as many as fifty grizzlies feeding together during the annual salmon run. Until Banff, Yellowstone and other national parks closed down their garbage dumps in the 1970s, similar congregations of grizzlies took advantage of these artificial concentrations of food.

Even when grizzlies congregate in spawning areas or at garbage dumps, there is an obvious hierarchy, with smaller or younger bears usually giving way to the dominant bears and settling for the least desirable feeding stations.

Gardener of the wilds

A grizzly's long claws and massive shoulder hump aren't weapons. They're digging tools. Like badgers, pocket gophers and other animals that move a lot of soil, grizzlies have long, slightly curved claws and muscular forelegs.

When a grizzly discovers a good root crop, it can move an impressive amount of earth. In Kootenay National Park's Honeymoon Pass, I once found a glacier lily patch that had recently been excavated by a grizzly. Rich black soil, like a freshly rototilled garden, covered a continuous area of close to a quarter hectare. Along the upper Yarrow Creek valley, near Pincher Creek, grizzlies digging for the roots of sweetvetch left barely any undisturbed ground along almost a kilometre of valley bottom.

Grizzlies leave behind fragments of roots and bulbs when feeding. These then regenerate and produce future crops, much like when gardeners divide perennials.

Grizzlies disturb so much land when feeding that they probably play an important role in creating habitat for plants like dandelion, sweetvetch and strawberry that prefer cultivated soil and little competition from other plants.

Grizzly foods

What plants do grizzlies prefer? It varies from one area to another depending on what is available; biologist Chris Servheen identified 165 different plant and animal species used by grizzlies in just one part of the Rocky Mountains. Some of the most important plants:

Dandelion Taraxacum officinale.

Sweetvetch
Hedysarum spp.

Skunk cabbage
Lysichitum
americanum.

Glacier lily
Erythronium
grandiflorum.

Tufted hairgrass
Deschampsia
cespitosa.

Buffaloberry
Shepherdia
canadensis.

Mountain fireweed
Epilobium
latifolium.

Moths on the menu

In the early 1990s, researchers Steve and Marilynn French observed up to twenty-four bears at one time, high in the jumbled scree above timberline in Yellowstone National Park, digging into the alpine slopes. The grizzlies were feeding on army cutworm moths, which congregate in large numbers in crevices and rubble. Prior to this discovery, biologists had believed whitebark pine seeds were the most important summer food source for the area's grizzlies. Grizzlies have since been spotted feeding on moths as far north as the Waterton-Glacier International Peace Park.

Catch-and-release for grizzlies

When catch-and-release angling was made law in Yellowstone National Park, few people were thinking about whether grizzly bears might benefit. Native Yellowstone cutthroat trout, however, increased under the new protective regulations to the point that they became an important seasonal food for bears.

In 1960 only 3,800 cutthroats spawned in Clear Creek, a tributary of Yellowstone Lake. Thirty years later there were over fifty thousand cutthroats spawning in the same creek late in June and early July. The increased number of fish led grizzlies to focus in on a newly important food source. Biologists say the great bears fished in only 41 streams in the 1960s, but by the end of the century they were hunting spawning cutthroats in at least 130 streams.

The boom was short-lived, however. In 1995 park authorities were horrified to discover that someone had illegally stocked non-native lake trout into Yellowstone Lake. Competition and predation has led to a crash in numbers of cutthroats. Since lake trout spawn in lakes rather than tributary streams, they are unavailable to hungry bears or the many other species that historically relied on cutthroats as food.

THE GRIZZLY BEAR THROUGH THE SEASONS

Early in April, grizzlies awaken from their winter's sleep and venture out of their dens into the blinding glare of spring sunlight on snow. Snow still blankets western Canada's high mountain slopes, but avalanches thunder all through the spring afternoons as the sun's growing warmth loosens the snow pack and sends it crashing down gullies into the valleys below. Coastal grizzlies find a milder reception, especially along low-elevation river valleys.

Grizzly tracks in snow.

The bears are hungry but food is scarce. Most trees and shrubs won't leaf out for another month, and only at the lowest elevations is the grass beginning to green up.

Spring grizzlies gravitate to sunny, south-facing slopes or the banks of low-elevation creeks and rivers. There, where snow has melted away from last year's brown, matted grasses, their sensitive noses sniff out the odour of sweetvetch roots, glacier lily bulbs and other buried treasures. Grizzlies efficiently uproot these starch-rich foods with their long claws, powered by massive shoulder muscles. Coastal bears feed on the roots of skunk cabbage and sedges or, where they can find them, the well-cured carcasses of salmon that died the previous fall after spawning.

The grizzlies' noses continually test the breeze for the promise of heartier fare. Late winter is a time of death for deer, elk, bighorn sheep and other animals. Some get caught and killed by spring avalanches, while others melt out of drifts where they had been buried by the winter snows. For a hungry grizzly, roots are fine but carrion is a jackpot.

The snowpack diminishes and the days lengthen. New greenery begins to sprout. The bears continue to dig roots and bulbs around the shrinking snowdrifts, but now they begin to add highly nutritious young grasses, horsetails and other sprouting vegetation to their diet.

By late May, glacier lilies, sweetvetch and other plants that were rich in stored energy no longer appeal to the bears, because the starch stored in roots and bulbs has gone into producing new stems, leaves and flowers. Now, however, the grizzlies are surrounded with a lush variety of young greenery. Life is one endless salad, interrupted by the occasional duck nest, ground squirrel or other side dish.

Deer, elk, moose and other ungulates give birth in late May and early June. Some grizzlies become skilled at hunting the newborns. I watched a grizzly hunting elk calves in Waterton Lakes National Park one morning. The bear coursed back and forth through aspen forest at a full run, like a bird dog, evidently trying to flush the calves his nose told him were hidden there.

In some areas, spawning trout, suckers or salmon congregate in shallow riffles, offering another concentrated, energy-rich food supply. Most grizzlies, however, continue to eat vegetation, insects and whatever other readily found foods cross their paths.

Low-elevation vegetation begins to cure by early summer, and its food value drops. In response, grizzlies concentrate on wetland areas along streams, or move to higher elevations where the vegetation remains lush later in the year. Insect populations continue to build through the summer; by July ant colonies in rotting logs and old stumps offer rich sources of protein. Later in the year, wasp nests become available under cutbanks and in rodent holes.

By mid-summer most grizzlies are at high elevations or on sheltered slopes, where they can both avoid heat and find lush vegetation. The long, warm days of summer have worked their magic on the low shrubbery of burns, avalanche slopes, snowbed areas and river floodplains, however, and berries are beginning to ripen.

Late July, most years, signals an important change in grizzly diets. Saskatoon berries, huckleberries, raspberries, salmonberries – a seasonal embarrassment of riches offers the great bears a concentrated supply of high-energy food that lasts until after the first frosts in September.

A prolonged drought or a wet, cold summer may result in a berry crop failure. This is bad news for bears because there are few alternative foods that offer anywhere near as much nutrition value. During bad years, grizzlies may wander widely in search of food. Some end up in marginal habitat, often in ranching country or around the edges of towns. Mortality is high and females produce few cubs the following spring.

By the time berry season is winding down, the mountains are gold and brown with fading foliage. Sweetvetch, glacier lily, spring beauty and other plants are dying back, having replenished the stores of starches and sugars in their roots, bulbs and corms. Once again, interior grizzlies begin to rototill the river banks and avalanche meadows, eating roots as other food supplies diminish. Fat families of ground squirrels and marmots are also available – more work to dig up, but more rewarding than roots. In many parts of their range, grizzlies will also feed on the year's crop of whitebark pine nuts in timberline forests. Coastal bears gravitate to salmon spawning areas.

Where hunting is allowed, late fall yields another rich food supply in the form of gut piles left behind by elk and deer hunters.

Late in November, most grizzlies weigh almost a third more than they did when they awoke in April. Energy-rich fat is caked beneath thick winter hides as grizzlies occupying the interior mountains and plateaus head for the high slopes to excavate winter dens. They commonly choose den sites on north- or east-facing aspects near the tops of mountain slopes. Snow accumulates on these lee slopes all through the winter, ensuring good insulation for the sleeping bears. With the first heavy snow of November drifting into their big, pigeon-toed tracks, the grizzlies squeeze into their dens and settle down for another winter's sleep.

Coastal grizzlies, on the other hand, more commonly seek out old-growth forests. Their winter enemy is endless rain, and a common solution is to find a large old red cedar tree whose core has rotted out. The big bears curl up inside the tree and sleep away the wet, dreary coastal winter. In the boreal forests and foothills of western Alberta and northeastern BC, grizzlies may excavate dens under uprooted trees or on sheltered hillsides that accumulate winter snow cover.

Too many what?

Grizzly populations have dropped from an estimated fifty thousand in 1850 to fewer than two thousand today in the continental United States. The change in Canada has been less dramatic, but the long-term trend is the same.

Most large mammals have decreased. One that hasn't is *Homo sapiens*. The human population of Canada stood at 2.4 million in 1850, when grizzlies still ranged as far east as Regina. By 1950 there were seven times as many people and perhaps half as many grizzlies.

Today, with well over thirty million humans crowding the landscape, the grizzly is threatened throughout most of its surviving range.

What is a viable population of grizzlies?

Conservation biologists say that for a population of bears or other animals to be considered viable, there must be a 95 per cent statistical probability that it will still be there a hundred years from now.

Based on that definition, scientists have built mathematical models for various sizes of theoretical bear populations. Models feed on data, but they are built of assumptions, so one scientist's model may give a different result from another.

A mother grizzly and her yearling cubs.

Since only some of the bear population is of breeding age at any given time, Steve Herrero and Wayne McCrory have calculated that a viable population would contain about four hundred grizzlies. The International Union for Conservation of Nature has established a threshold number of one thousand, below which long-term viability is at risk. Based on this threshold, in 2010 the Province of Alberta declared its grizzly population of only seven hundred bears threatened. Lee Metzgar, on the other hand, estimates that Montana and Idaho would need at least two thousand bears before they have a viable population.

Small, isolated populations are at risk from several factors:

1. *Genetic inbreeding*: the smaller the population, the more likely that related bears will mate with each other. Inbreeding causes abnormalities that can increase the death rate and produce offspring less fertile than their parents.

2. *Genetic drift*: the smaller the variety of genes in a population, the more chance that some of those genes will be lost when individual bears die, resulting in a bear population increasingly different from and less robust than the rest of the species.

3. *Chance disasters*: if a major storm, fire, disease or other event kills a large number of bears, a small population may not be able to recover. This isn't a problem where grizzlies from other areas can find their way into the affected area, but it's a big problem for the isolated populations that are typical of the northern US and southern Canada.

Dead-end roads and grizzly dams

A road is often the beginning of the end for grizzly bears.

Grizzlies die regularly on the pavement of Montana's Interstate 15. The World Wildlife Fund has identified Canada's Highway 3, which slices across the Rocky and Selkirk Mountains just north of the US border, as one of the biggest threats to the long-term survival of grizzly populations in northern Montana and Idaho. Vehicle collisions kill bears. So do poachers, who find bears more easily along roads.

But roads are deadly for a more insidious reason too: they attract development. Uncontrolled land development along major roadways results in "grizzly dams" – ecological no-go zones along the valleys that separate mountain ranges. Commercial strips, towns and recreational subdivisions along highways fragment bear ranges.

A single mountain range may support only fifteen to twenty bears. This is no problem as long as bears can cross the intervening valleys safely and mate with other bears nearby. Once humans take over the valleys, however, grizzlies can no longer live safely there, even though the valleys are usually the most productive bear habitat. Grizzlies that don't avoid roads and habitations often end up dead. Pockets of bears become isolated in small populations in the safe, but less productive, high-mountain habitat.

"All these mountain valleys [in the American Northwest] are being developed," says Chris Servheen. "All have these kinds of problems."

Servheen coordinates the Grizzly Bear Recovery Team, a group established under the US Endangered Species Act to recover the grizzly in the Rocky Mountain states. He warns that northern Montana, western

Alberta and southern BC will lose more grizzly populations if development along valley-bottom road corridors continues at the current rate.

The executive director of the Northern Rockies Conservation Cooperative predicted in 1995 that development would actually accelerate. "Trillions of dollars are forecast to pass into the hands of baby boomers in the next ten years," Peyton Curlee said. "We're forecasting a doubling of subdivisions and recreational second homes as a direct consequence." She was right. Strip development and monster homes are now the norm in what used to be grizzly country.

Servheen says, "When we look at the distribution of grizzlies in the northern US Rockies, we see what we see for other carnivores. They extend down in these island-like, or isthmus-like, populations. The low-elevation boundaries aren't habitat-related, they're human-related ... We've excluded these creatures from their best habitat in most of their North American range."

Farther north, the heavily travelled Trans-Canada Highway formed a grizzly dam across the Rocky Mountains in Banff and Yoho National Parks until Parks Canada invested millions of dollars to construct overpasses and underpasses for wildlife. East of the park, however, the town of Canmore's urban sprawl has nearly filled the same valley. Increasing highway traffic volumes combined with recreational real estate development is building more such dams in southern BC and Alberta.

Grizzly populations isolated behind these ecological dams will continue to expire one by one, says Chris Servheen, unless we give bears secure ways to range throughout the landscape. Most conservation biologists call for large wilderness preserves connected by secure

corridors of habitat – including highway-crossing structures – and surrounded by sensitively managed forest
and ranching areas that are out of bounds not for bears
but for real estate speculators.

Grizzlies and clear-cuts

Logging isn't necessarily bad for bears. The whine of
chainsaws and the rumble of logging trucks barely dis-
turbed the slumbers of some of the bears Bruce McLellan
studied in southeast British Columbia's Flathead River
valley during the 1980s. On a few occasions McLellan
found radio-collared grizzlies bedded down within a few
hundred metres of active logging operations.

McLellan's study grizzlies had a few things in their
favour, however, that helped them cope with logging
activity. The Flathead valley has some of the most productive grizzly habitats in the Rocky Mountains. Bears
range across a virtually uninhabited landscape that
includes many roadless areas and, south of the international border, a large protected wilderness in Montana's
Glacier National Park. And the logging activities that
McLellan observed were the first pass; loggers were
removing only a small portion of the available forest.

Farther north, loggers were doing their second pass
through the headwaters of the Kootenay and Beaverfoot
Rivers, an area that lies between Yoho and Kootenay
National Parks. When they finished, well more than
half the area's merchantable timber had been cleared.
Grizzly populations in that area are under growing stress

A mother and her older cub engaging in bonding behaviour.

as the amount of forest cover shrinks and the number of kilometres of open road increases each year.

McLellan's research showed that unless logging roads are physically closed and reclaimed as soon as the work is finished, commercial logging in grizzly country reduces habitat security for grizzlies. Hunting pressure increases and a growing number of fishermen, huckleberry-pickers and other recreationists take advantage of the new logging roads to penetrate deep into once-remote areas where their presence displaces bears or triggers conflicts that result in dead grizzlies.

Some forestry agencies now insist that logging companies close and reclaim their roads to protect grizzlies and other animals from conflict with people, but off-road vehicle users often find a way to reopen the roads and turn them into unauthorized trails.

Burn a grizzly in your furnace this winter
Any thinking consumer can see Mike Sawyer's point. But his fellow Albertans often vilify him, because they consider any criticism of the oil and gas industry to be close to treason.

Nothing daunted, Sawyer and other members of the Rocky Mountain Ecosystem Coalition continue to assemble information about the effects of oil and gas exploration and drilling on the grizzlies and other animals that depend upon western Alberta's diminishing wilderness. Then they lay that information before

A grizzly's long claws make it adept at digging for roots, vegetation and insects.

regulatory panels, the media and natural gas consumers throughout the Pacific Northwest.

Oil and gas exploration involves the cutting of temporary roads across the landscape, oblivious to streams, ridges or bogs. Exploration crews use tracked or balloon-wheeled vehicles to traverse these cutlines, discharging blasts of explosive at regular intervals to evaluate the underlying geology.

Companies guard their seismic data jealously, so several energy companies often end up visiting the same area. Rob McManus of the Canadian Association of Petroleum Producers reported that energy companies were cutting an average of thirty-nine thousand miles of seismic lines each year by the late twentieth century. He describes the result as "seismic spaghetti." Most Alberta bear country now looks, from the air, as if it has been flayed by dozens of whips. Seismic lines criss-cross the forest in all directions.

Once a company gets promising results from its seismic surveys, it applies for the right to drill exploratory wells. Wells require more substantial roads than seismic surveys, and if the company finds petroleum reserves, it builds high-quality industrial roads that become virtually permanent features of the landscape. The energy industry has drilled close to two hundred thousand oil and gas wells in Alberta already, with ninety thousand more approved in the first decade of the twentieth century.

Sawyer points to the Shell-Waterton gas field southwest of Pincher Creek as an example of the impacts of incremental gas development. Virtually every creek valley in the area celebrated in Andy Russell's classic *Grizzly Country* now has at least one high-quality gravel road and several wells and pipelines. As recently as the fall of 1995, poachers used one of the roads to kill a grizzly bear that had taken up temporary residence in a large berry patch. Sawyer says such events are inevitable as long as natural gas consumers and governments don't hold the petroleum industry accountable for restoring grizzly habitat and leaving wilderness areas unimpaired by industrial activity.

Canadian regulatory agencies like the National Energy Board and Alberta's Energy Resources Conservation Board continue to stonewall Sawyer and other environmentalists. While paying lip service to the needs of grizzly bears, they approve virtually every well application, pipeline submission and gas export permit that comes before them.

Backyard bears

In the North Fork of Montana's Flathead River, researchers have found that most of the grizzlies living near the valley's farms and homes are young. But they don't know how many of those young bears survive to old age.

If young grizzlies, which older males often attack, can find security near humans, then a low level of human development may actually help grizzly populations, as long as the human community is willing to help the bears stay out of trouble.

But if residents expose bears to the temptation of garbage and easily killed livestock, or if poachers kill the readily accessible bears, the developed valley bottoms become mortality sinks – a sort of black hole for grizzly bears. This appears to be the situation in the North Fork valley, judging from the number of "problem" bears trapped or killed there each year.

A grizzly explores its home range.

Field and Sissy

Two young grizzlies followed their mother into the small town of Field, BC, in the late 1980s. The sibling bears soon became popular with town residents, who named them Field and Sissy. Field and Sissy foraged with their mother along the forest fringes and avalanche slopes near town.

Researchers captured the bear family and fitted them with radio collars, along with eight other grizzly bears ranging through the protected wilderness of Yoho and Kootenay National Parks. The biologists hoped to learn where the most important bear habitats were so that park managers could protect them from too much human use.

Field and Sissy, however, chose to spend a lot of their time in and around the town of Field, especially after their mother died in the spring of 1991. Residents often came across the young grizzlies on side streets or along the road out of town. The bears always minded their own business, eating dandelions and lawn grasses and showing no signs of aggression.

Then, in 1992, Field happened across a bowl of dog food someone had left on a back porch. Next he found some food in a compost bin. The familiar cycle had begun. Field moved to the Lake O'Hara area and found food in a campground, finally becoming so persistent that park wardens trapped him and shipped him to remote northern Alberta. There he raided the kitchen of an oil camp, and provincial conservation officers finally killed him.

Sissy avoided food temptation, but she became fatally comfortable with people and vehicles. She began feeding regularly along the Icefields Parkway, delighting many tourists with her peaceful demeanour. But her affinity for roads was her downfall. One day she stepped in front of a Brewster tour bus and was killed.

In all, eight of the eleven radio-collared study bears died within three years. Besides Sissy and Field, hunters killed two, using logging roads to penetrate the once-remote forests west of Yoho. Poachers apparently killed another, and two died of unknown causes. That rate of mortality, if it reflects the trend in the rest of the population, indicates a grizzly bear population on a fast track to oblivion.

It was the deaths of Field and Sissy, however, that most troubled the conservation-minded community of Field, which had, too briefly, lived in harmony with the bears. When Sissy died, the townspeople held a memorial service in her honour.

Rocky Mountain dynasty

Almost every grizzly in the central Canadian Rockies is descended from the same female – evidence of a remarkable genetic bottleneck in the population, says Mike Gibeau.

Gibeau's analysis of DNA from over thirty bears showed that genetic diversity is still fairly high, probably because wide-ranging male grizzlies have bred with local females. But it is lower than other northern grizzly populations and comparable to grizzlies at the very edge of their natural range.

This sort of information has helped Gibeau and other biologists identify the real conservation priorities for the grizzlies that range through Banff, Kananaskis Country and the east slopes of Alberta's Rocky Mountains. His findings suggest that the population cannot afford to lose any females – disconcerting news, since Banff National Park alone has lost more than one female grizzly per year, mostly to train collisions, over the past decade.

Since males seem to be the source of the population's genetic diversity, Gibeau says that land use planning needs to ensure that male bears can range safely over wide areas. This would increase the odds of bears from the central Rockies breeding with bears from other areas.

Genetic diversity is important, says Gibeau, because it ensures bears can adapt to change.

THREATS TO GRIZZLIES

Grizzly bears need space. With more than half a billion human beings on this continent, most of the space they need is occupied, or used, by us.

Grizzly bears need so much space that even the big western national parks and wilderness areas can't meet their needs. The parks really aren't as big or as wild as we like to think they are. For example, more than eight thousand people live year-round in Banff National Park, and another five million visit the park each year to use facilities, trails and resorts that take up space no longer available to the great bears.

A surprised grizzly stands up for a better view.

So the conservation problem has two dimensions. On the one hand, a lot of grizzly bear habitat has been permanently lost to cities, resorts, intensive agriculture and pavement, while more continues to be lost every year. And on the other hand, much of the good habitat that remains – national parks, large ranches, forestry areas – is no longer as friendly to grizzlies, because conflict with humans too often results in the death of bears. The habitat is there; it's just not a secure place for a bear to be.

It's important to clearly distinguish between these two dimensions of the conservation problem – habitat loss and habitat security – in order to find workable solutions for each. Strategies to protect grizzly bear habitat won't work without parallel efforts to improve habitat security. Both require different tactics. And both are compounded by global changes that are affecting grizzly bear food sources.

Habitat loss

The history of western North America has been one of putting the landscape to work. Where the climate and soils would support agricultural crops, natural ecosystems have been turned into farmland with little or no room for grizzlies. Productive forest areas have been dedicated to the production of wood, while grassland areas are given over to the production of beef. Even the high mountains, where most large parks and wilderness areas exist, are expected to contribute to the economy through tourism revenues.

Wide-ranging animals like grizzlies face a double-edged sword. On the one hand, they need large tracts of habitat. And on the other hand, even if habitat is abundant, the conversion of even a very small area to other human uses can create an ecological black hole where bears that range over a much larger area die because of conflict with humans. Regional garbage dumps are an example of such a black hole. The Canadian Pacific rail line through Banff and Yoho National Parks is another example, killing bears that travel from the surrounding mountains to forage for spilled grain, peas and other agricultural products that leak from rail cars.

Recognizing the critical importance of stopping – or even reversing – the tide of habitat loss that has driven grizzlies out of most of their former North American range, conservation groups, wildlife agencies and land management planners have begun looking for new ways to protect habitat. Conservation groups actively promote land use planning to keep grizzly populations in the northern US Rockies from becoming cut off from adjacent areas of grizzly habitat. Large ranches and private forestry holdings can be valuable grizzly habitat, but it isn't economical for conservation groups to try and purchase them outright. Instead, groups like Nature Conservancy of Canada and the Vital Ground Foundation rely on conservation easements, purchase of development rights and other innovative real estate transactions to keep bear habitat from being subdivided or developed outside of parks and protected wilderness areas.

Habitat security
There is a deadness about a landscape that should hold grizzlies but doesn't. Something vital is missing. Aldo Leopold described such a place in New Mexico:

"Escudilla still hangs on the horizon, but when you see it you no longer think of bear. It's only a mountain now."

Across western North America there are many such landscapes where grizzly bear foods are plentiful, the human population sparse, wild space abundant – but there are no longer any grizzlies. In some parts of the West, grizzlies persist, but far fewer than the available habitat could support.

Conservation biologists use the term "habitat security" to describe the degree to which human activity or development displaces animals from what would otherwise be good habitat. Generally, grizzly bear habitat is most secure when the bears can forage in peace. When human use of bear habitat increases the likelihood that repeated disturbance will cause bears to avoid the area, there's been a reduction of habitat security. Overall, that means the landscape will hold fewer bears.

Outside protected parks, habitat security declines when oil, gas and forestry companies cut roads into remote valleys, enabling poachers to find and kill bears that were previously protected by isolation. Mountain bikers and off-road vehicle enthusiasts can unwittingly displace bears when they cut new trails into isolated places.

Fortunately, it's possible to restore habitat security. Wayne McCrory and Erica Mallam, for example, helped BC Parks managers relocate campgrounds and reroute hiking trails out of high quality grizzly feeding areas to reduce conflict between hikers and bears. McCrory also teamed up with Steve Herrero to help

The scent or sound of humans can make wary bears avoid valuable habitat.

Alberta's Kananaskis Country managers make similar adjustments. Some logging and oil and gas companies have negotiated the right to close and lock their access roads on public lands, partly in order to protect vulnerable wildlife like grizzlies from disturbance. Conservationist Mike McIvor of Alberta's Bow Valley Naturalists believes that the only way Banff National Park can restore habitat security to heavily developed areas like the Bow valley would be to physically remove tourism facilities and prohibit human use of critical areas. Increasingly, however, Parks Canada has been experimenting with another way of improving habitat security – simply helping bears feel secure in places where they once weren't tolerated, using bear guardians to supervise the crowd at bear jams and ensure that nobody disturbs the bear. This approach, while costly, restores bear security not by removing development, but by reducing displacement.

Food losses

The most robust grizzly populations are those that can rely on high-quality food sources. For millennia, annual salmon-spawning runs supported some of the continent's largest grizzlies from Alaska to California. Dams killed many of those salmon runs in the twentieth century, especially in the Columbia River drainage, where salmon used to be able to migrate as far upstream as Radium Hot Springs. Grizzly bears vanished from the coastal watersheds of the US for several reasons – not just the loss of salmon but also the loss of their annual bonanza greatly reduced the carrying capacity of those places in the Columbia drainage where grizzlies persist.

Farther north, the Fraser River and other coastal

drainages escaped the ravages of the dam-builders. Their salmon populations are no longer assured, however. Global climate change appears to be altering the distribution of heat in the world's oceans, with the result that some salmon runs are no longer as reliable. Grizzlies travel long distances to hunt salmon in the Bella Coola and Atnarko Rivers, drainages where they historically caused few problems for the farms and settlements that line the rivers. When salmon runs failed in 2008 and 2009, however, desperate bears went looking for other food supplies. Conservation officers killed between twenty-five and thirty bears during that two-year period.

Climate change is compounding food problems for Yellowstone's grizzlies too. White pine blister rust, a fungal disease originating in Europe, hitched a ride to North America aboard currant bushes imported for fruit culture. Once here, the fungus spread to trees that had no defences against it. Among the most vulnerable of those trees, limber and whitebark pine produce oil-rich pine nuts that are a vital food source for grizzlies in Yellowstone and other high mountain areas.

More than 90 per cent of whitebark pines are now dead throughout much of their range, including the Waterton–Glacier International Peace Park. In the late twentieth century, it appeared that Yellowstone's pines were avoiding blister rust's ravages. But summer droughts are growing longer in the West, and winters have become milder. Those climate changes favour the spread of a native insect – the mountain pine beetle – that attacks and kills weakened trees. The combined effect of blister rust and pine beetles has been to decimate Yellowstone's pines.

Researchers had already noted that during years when pine nut production was low, more grizzly bears got into trouble searching for alternative food sources. The death of important food trees, combined with the loss of spawning cutthroat trout displaced by competition with non-native lake trout illegally released into Yellowstone Lake, is another blow against Yellowstone's recovering, but still endangered, grizzly population.

Official overkill?

"The Wildlife Branch, through allowance and mismanagement of grizzly quotas, has been participating in the process of local extinctions of grizzlies.

"There have been many studies by the Wildlife Branch, private consultants, Parks Canada and others that document very alarming mortality rates near areas where trophy hunting is permitted. The Wildlife Branch has set quotas for total human-caused mortalities of grizzlies at 4 per cent. In many areas they are simply allowing those quotas to be exceeded through inaction. A recent study near Kokanee Provincial Park showed that the Wildlife Branch's management allowed a third of the female grizzlies in the population to be wiped out.

"It makes no sense, when the grizzly bear has been listed as vulnerable, to continue to allow trophy hunting of the most slowly reproducing mammal in North America."

—Wayne McCrory, BC bear ecologist

HUNTING IN GRIZZLY COUNTRY

Grizzly bear hunting appeals to a small minority of hunters, many of whom are drawn to the activity more by their fantasies about the great bear than by any real understanding of bears or their habitat. Some see killing a grizzly as one of the ultimate hunting challenges, just as it has always been for some First Nations tribes. For too many, unfortunately, it is simply a way to win boasting rights by killing what they perceive as a dangerous adversary.

Regardless of hunter motivation, grizzly bears are not biologically suited to be prey species. They reproduce slowly, occupy huge home ranges and are slow to recover from losses to their populations. Where hunting is still permitted, wildlife agencies strive to keep annual human-caused grizzly deaths, including hunting, below 6 per cent of the total estimated bear population. Some biologists feel that even this conservative number is too high and that unnatural mortality from all causes, including hunting, needs to be kept below 4 per cent annually if grizzly populations are to survive.

Montana, Wyoming, Idaho and Washington no longer allow hunting, because the grizzly is protected under the Endangered Species Act. Alberta suspended its grizzly hunt in 2008 when a detailed population assessment showed there to be far fewer bears than had been assumed. Alberta's grizzlies were declared threatened in 2010 after scientific peer review confirmed the new population estimates.

Next door in British Columbia, however, sport hunting for grizzly bears continues through draws that allocate licences on a first-come, first-served basis to a limited number of hunters. BC hunters kill about three hundred grizzlies each year. Unlike most other provinces and states, where hunting is not allowed in protected areas, BC loses about 10 per cent of its hunter-killed grizzlies inside provincial parks. Successful hunters cannot apply for another licence until several years have passed. Unlike black bears, grizzly bears cannot legally be shot over bait.

Even though the kill rate may seem very low, hunting can have a long-lasting impact on bear populations – especially when hunters kill females. A government review in BC found that hunters were killing too many grizzlies in five out of eight management areas, and that the number of females killed exceeded the acceptable level in seven of those areas. Commercial outfitters and some rural politicians stubbornly defend the hunt, but most bear biologists argue that BC's Wildlife Branch should no longer allow any hunting of grizzly bears anywhere.

A controversial 1993 study challenged the prevalent belief by many bear managers that limited hunting is good for grizzly populations because it removes large adult males that often kill cubs. Robert Wielgus studied bear populations in Alberta's Kananaskis Valley and BC's Selkirk Range and came to the conclusion that killing adult males may actually work against the interests of cubs by allowing more young males – which the old, dominant males would otherwise have harassed or killed – to move into habitats used by females with cubs. The young males, Wielgus suspected, may kill as many or more cubs than the large, dominant males.

Hunting can even have an impact on grizzlies where bears aren't the target. When two hunters failed to return from a 1995 elk hunting trip near Invermere,

BC, searchers made an unwelcome discovery. A grizzly and her cubs had appropriated the carcass of an elk the hunters had shot and begun to clean. The mauled bodies of both hunters lay nearby, along with their guns and gear. Officials killed all three bears. Later that fall a grizzly killed another hunter farther south, and other elk hunters shot at least three grizzlies, ostensibly in self-defence. Pepper spray could have saved the bears and the hunters.

Grizzly bears in several regions have learned to home in on the sound of gunshots in hopes of a chance to fatten on the remains of hunters' kills. Yellowstone National Park is surrounded by important grizzly bear habitat controlled by the US Forest Service. Besides supporting grizzlies, the national forests contain abundant herds of elk and mule deer which, every fall, attract hunters from all across the country. Bear-versus-hunter conflicts are common.

Over the years, the Forest Service has instituted regulations to reduce the risk of hunters and bears coming into conflict, since most such conflicts end with a dead grizzly that the ecosystem cannot spare. Those regulations showed their teeth in 1988, when three Wyoming hunters killed a grizzly. They were fined $2,000 each when it was shown in court that they had hung elk meat near their tent and low to the ground. Forest Service regulations require that game meat be hung at least one hundred yards from camp and no less than three metres from the ground, for reasons that are obvious to experienced hunters in bear country.

Dick Knight, former head of the Interagency Grizzly Bear Study Team in the Yellowstone ecosystem, expresses impatience with hunters who kill grizzlies.

Describing them as "woods wimps," he says, "If they are afraid of bears they shouldn't hunt in grizzly country."

So-called self-defence kills of grizzly bears are, in fact, rarely justified. In too many cases naive hunters, having read too many bear horror stories for their own good, overreact to bluff charges or to the mere sight of a bear at close range. Many experienced hunters now carry pepper spray to improve the odds that both they and the bear will come out of a surprise encounter alive.

Trusting grizzlies

Charlie Russell is somewhat like a bear himself: a powerfully built, slow-speaking woodsman whose gentle manner exudes quiet intelligence.

Growing up on a cattle ranch north of Waterton Lakes National Park, Charlie became familiar with bears from a young age. He and his brothers helped his father, Andy, during the filming of *Grizzly Country*, and two of his brothers went on to become professional biologists.

Charlie, on the other hand, chose a naturalistic approach to the study of the big animals that, in many ways, have taken over his entire life. He spends extended periods of time among bears, getting to know them as individuals and observing their behaviour with one another as well as with him.

For several years in the 1990s, Charlie worked as a guide for Tom Ellison and Jenny Broom, bringing small groups of tourists by boat to the estuary wetlands of Khutzeymateen Inlet. Among the bears he got to know through repeated visits to the area's sedge marshes and old growth forests was a mother grizzly who became so comfortable with him that, as he describes in the preamble to one of his books, one day she actually sat down beside him and touched his hand. During the Khutzeymateen years, Charlie helped filmmakers Jeff and Sue Turner document the remarkable white-phase "spirit" bears of Princess Royal Island. Again, he formed strong bonds of friendship with several individual bears.

Charlie's experience with the trusting bears of BC's coastal wildernesses fed a growing suspicion that wild-life management agencies and people living in bear country were basing their interactions with bears on assumptions that are dead wrong. Determined to prove, if only to himself, that humans and bears could live together with respect, mutual trust and even friendship, he looked for a piece of bear country so remote that the bears there would not yet have been spoiled by too much of the wrong kind of exposure to humans.

He found that place on the Kamchatka Peninsula, in Russia. It was in 1996 that he and Maureen Enns began

Charlie Russell and Biscuit relax beside a wilderness lake.

their decade-long adventure amid one of the highest densities of grizzly bears on the planet. Over several years, Charlie rescued captive bear cubs from Russian zoos and flew them to his cabin near Kambalnoye Lake, where he would then spend the ensuing months teaching them to forage and fend for themselves in a landscape full of salmon, berries, nut pines ... and dozens of other bears.

The first few years of the Kamchatka experience are documented in a book Charlie co-authored with Maureen Enns: *Grizzly Heart, Living without Fear among the Brown Bears of Kamchatka*. A remarkable BBC documentary, *The Edge of Eden: Living with Grizzlies*, documents one of his final seasons among the bears of Kamchatka.

"I trusted virtually all the bears there," says Charlie. "If I knew them for a while, I could trust them. And the females were some of the best. They were the ones that, once they trusted, they really trusted. They were in your hip pocket. They liked their cubs around me, and they would leave them to be babysat, things like that."

Although Charlie's experiences among the Kamchatka bears confirmed for him that our fear of bears stands between us and a far more enriching and sustaining relationship with them, he remains troubled by the question of how to build trust between species in the crowded landscapes of North America's bear country. While recognizing that some individual bears can be dangerous, he is convinced that there would be fewer bear conflicts if people treated the animals with more humility and respect:

"What I decided was that bears become dangerous for a reason. Even the bears that don't know people can be dangerous. When they get old they become compromised, just like we do, and because they have to survive over the winter – which is an amazing feat – eventually they can't do that. Every bear eventually can't get fat enough to survive a winter and that's usually when they die. So they get desperate. And I've been around those bears, and those bears can be really scary. They just start looking on people like anything else, for the possibility of food.

"But that is so rare. Even a bear like that is pretty easy to scare out of trouble.

"What we can do in order to improve the odds is just quit being rough with them. I think that our management of them is too violent, too rough. If that's the only experience bears have of people, then they're not going to trust us. And we need them to trust us because you want those female bears with cubs not to look at everyone as trouble. Because then, if those bears are surprised, knowing how protective they are, well, it can be tricky and dangerous."

KEEPING SAFE IN GRIZZLY COUNTRY

Writing about the last grizzly killed in Arizona's White Mountains, almost three-quarters of a century ago, Aldo Leopold said, "It must be poor life that achieves freedom from fear."

In fact, however, there is very little cause for fear in grizzly country. Statistics show that domestic dogs, bees and lightning are all more dangerous. The likelihood of even seeing a grizzly is very small; if you see a grizzly, the chances that it will be aggressive are very small; and

Grizzlies intently feeding on berries can be dangerous if surprised.

if a grizzly actually charges, the chances of the charge becoming an attack are even more minuscule. Grizzlies avoid conflict with us at least as much as we try to avoid conflict with them.

Even so, many people let fear of a grizzly attack keep them from venturing out into the woods and mountains. It shouldn't be that way.

One way to deal with fear is to visit places where there are no more grizzlies. Campers and hikers can enjoy grizzly-free scenery in Saskatchewan's Cypress Hills, the Colorado Rockies, California's Sierra Nevada or Utah's Uinta Mountains. Leopold's "poor life" is widely available.

Another solution is simply to stay home. If you get mugged, at least it won't be by a bear.

But fear doesn't have to shut anyone out of bear country. You can learn enough about grizzlies to travel confidently in the places where they live. A few common-sense precautions, along with an informed understanding of how and why grizzly attacks occur, go a long way toward converting fear into watchful caution.

Considering the size and strength of a grizzly bear, it's surprising they don't consider us food – but they don't. Predatory attacks by grizzlies are even rarer than those by black bears. As mentioned earlier, the powerful shoulder hump and long claws of a grizzly are not weaponry; they are digging tools. Grizzlies use them to excavate roots, bulbs, rodents and other subterranean goodies.

Because of their large size and long digging claws, grizzlies are poorly suited for climbing trees. Unlike black bears, which instinctively climb trees when threatened, grizzlies have to find another way of responding to any potential threat from another bear or a human. Grizzlies are also more of an open country animal than black bears; even if they were inclined to climb trees, there's no guarantee they can always find one in easy reach.

Steve Herrero has reviewed the circumstances around all major bear attacks in the last century. His research shows that the vast majority of attacks involved bears surprised at close quarters. They attacked in self-defence, out of fear.

The conclusion is obvious: avoid surprising a grizzly. Be alert, put the wind at your back when possible, and move slowly, making plenty of noise, when visibility is poor because of dense vegetation or where there is a lot of noise from water or wind. Watch for fresh diggings, tracks or other bear signs. Avoid those areas or, if there's no choice, move through them slowly and noisily. If you see a gathering of ravens or magpies, or if you smell decomposition, there may be a dead animal nearby with a grizzly feeding on it. Stay well away.

If you do surprise a bear, there is still a good chance you can defuse the situation by reassuring it that you aren't a threat. Turn aside, lower your head, talk gently and make it clear that you mean the bear no harm. At the same time, get your pepper spray handy just in case.

When a grizzly feels threatened, its first line of defence is often a threat display or bluff charge. Startled grizzlies may clack their teeth, turn sideways to show their body size, or make sudden, short rushes at their adversary. If bluffing doesn't work, however, and the stakes are high enough, a grizzly may attack and try to injure its opponent. When are the stakes highest for a grizzly? When a mother has cubs to protect, when a bear has laid claim to a valuable food source such as a carcass or when a bear feels cornered.

Chances are you won't even need your bear spray. But when in grizzly country, always carry bear spray where you can reach it in a hurry. It is a last and highly effective line of defence. The aerosol-propelled preparation is meant to be sprayed in front of a charging bear. The active ingredient, a derivative of capsicum pepper, causes instant, painful inflammation of exposed mucus membranes in the eye, nose or mouth, but causes no lasting damage. Pepper spray is easier to deploy than a firearm and accuracy isn't as critical; the spray comes out in a spreading cloud and it doesn't take much of it to have an effect. Bears hit with pepper spray virtually always retreat immediately.

The great advantage of pepper spray over firearms is that it applies training theory perfectly: it punishes the unwanted behaviour. The next time that bear encounters a human, the odds of an attack will be lower. Pepper spray, in other words, keeps both humans and bears alive.

Know how to use it. Keep it handy at all times. Even when hunting for my annual supply of elk or deer meat each fall, I carry pepper spray on my waist-strap. I know that it's a far better bear defence than the rifle slung over my shoulder.

Some macho types scoff at pepper spray, preferring to carry a firearm in grizzly country. Bad idea. A poorly placed bullet can turn a harmless bluff charge into a deadly attack by a wounded bear. I shared a hospital room one night with a rancher who had shot himself in the leg with a pistol he carried for bear protection. Ironically it was not a bear but his gun that put him in hospital. Many bears have died unnecessarily simply because someone packing a gun got scared.

There is still a risk of not being able to use bear spray in time to stop a charge, so pepper spray is no substitute for alertness and intelligent caution. Bear spray doesn't make you invincible.

If, in spite of everything, a grizzly actually attacks you, most grizzly experts advise lying face-down on the ground, covering your head and neck, and playing dead. Grizzlies tend to focus defensive attacks on the head area. Once a grizzly feels you are no longer a threat, he or she will generally retreat.

Reduce the risk of a grizzly conflict:

- Carry capsicum-pepper bear spray and always keep it ready to hand.

- Make noise in places where visibility is poor, so that you don't surprise a grizzly at such close range that it feels threatened. The best noise is an occasional high-pitched yell. That irritating little tinkle of bear bells is virtually useless because the sound does not carry far.

- For the same reason, try and keep the wind at your back when you can; let any bears in the area smell you before you arrive.

- Check with local park or wildlife authorities to find out if bears are likely to be in the area.

- Know where bears are likely to be at the season when you are hiking (but recognize that bears can be almost anywhere). Learn to recognize seasonal bear foods.

- Be alert and read the landscape; be conscious of the potential for surprising a bear as vegetation and terrain change.

- If you smell a rotting carcass in the area or see ravens circling, retreat downwind or make a wide detour, shouting frequently. Never approach anything dead.

- Campers should keep all food and garbage inside a closed vehicle or, if in the backcountry, in sealed plastic containers suspended at least three metres above the ground and well away from where you sleep.

- If establishing a long-stay camp or holding livestock and their feed in the backcountry, use portable electric fencing to deter curious bears from following their noses into trouble.

Bear spray and body language

Charlie Russell, who has probably spent as much time at close quarters with wild bears as anyone, is a strong believer in the importance of capsicum-pepper-based bear sprays. In his work with orphaned bear cubs in Kamchatka, Charlie had to use the spray on several occasions to stop predatory male bears from attacking the cubs he was working with. It always worked.

He feels that the real benefit of the spray, however, is the confidence it gives the person carrying it.

"Bears really react to our body language," he says. "When you're calm, it calms the bear too. Having bear spray helps people be less tense around bears.

"It's very important to keep it very handy, not tucked away in some pocket in your pack."

7
POLAR BEAR

Euarctos arctos maritimus

Polar bears grow bigger than any other bear in the world. Their elongated shape and small head give polar bears a distinctly different profile than other North American bear species. And polar bears, unlike black bears and grizzlies, are truly predatory; meat makes up more than 90 per cent of their diet.

Polar bear facts

Length	1.5–3 m (6–11 ft.)
Weight	300–550 kg (660–1,200 lb.)
Description	White, elongated body with a small head; tallest at the hind end.
Reproduction	First breeds at 4–7 years; has 1–3 cubs every three or more years.
Lifespan	25–30 years.
Diet	Primarily meat.
Distribution	Arctic coast; Arctic and North Atlantic Oceans, Hudson Bay.

Unlike grizzlies and black bears,
polar bears hunt throughout the winter.

Polar bears hunt seals and other marine mammals on the pack ice all through the long Arctic Ocean winter, heading inshore as summer approaches. The big bears concentrate along the coast after the pack ice breaks up in June and July, then head back out to sea as the ice begins to form again late in the fall.

Pregnant females, however, can't continue to hunt like the rest of the population. They remain inland, digging a den up to three metres deep in a convenient snowdrift. There, in a chamber that sits a bit higher than the entrance hole so that it will hold rising body heat, the mother gives birth to as many as three cubs sometime in December or January.

Polar bear milk is the richest milk of any of the bears, containing from 35 to 45 per cent fat. A regular diet of seals probably has a lot to do with this, since marine mammals have heavy layers of insulating fat inside their hides. In any case, the cubs fatten and grow quickly, following their mother out of the den in March.

One of the largest concentrations of polar bears in the world is near Churchill, Manitoba, on the southeast shoreline of Hudson Bay. An estimated 150 to 200 adult females den in the coastal drainages between Churchill and old York Factory and along the south side of Hudson Bay west of James Bay.

Adult males can be up to four times larger than females. As is the case with other bear species, males are aggressive predators of bear cubs and smaller bears. Biologists speculate that this may be why pregnant females often migrate up to forty kilometres inland; by denning in marginal habitat the females avoid the big males that congregate on the best habitat, closer to the coastline.

Canada's polar bears are part of an interconnected population that extends all around the north polar region of the planet, rather than being confined just to one continent. The polar bear specialists group of the International Union for Conservation of Nature recognizes nineteen distinct polar bear subpopulations, of which eight are declining in numbers and only one is increasing.

Canada's subpopulations are among those in the most trouble. The western Hudson Bay population dropped by 22 per cent in the early 1980s, likely because earlier ice breakup means they have had to stop hunting seals earlier each year. Changes in sea ice are further compounded by overhunting of the Baffin Bay population, which lives in both Canada and Greenland; meanwhile, polar bears in the Southern Beaufort Sea population are showing lower cub survival rates and reduced body weight among adults – signs that preceded the rapid population decline in the Hudson Bay area.

Is the polar bear a grizzly?

A guided hunter on Banks Island, Northwest Territories, killed a strange-looking bear in April 2006. Although its creamy-white fur made it look like a polar bear, its humped back, dish-shaped face and patches of brown on its head were suspiciously grizzly-like. The hunter was licensed to kill a polar bear, but he faced a big fine if it turned out he'd shot a grizzly.

DNA analysis eventually confirmed he'd actually shot both. The hybrid bear had a polar bear mother and a grizzly bear father. Four years later, an Inuvialuit hunter shot another hybrid. This one's DNA showed that its mother had been a hybrid too.

Biologists, who normally consider two kinds of similar animals to be separate species if they can't reproduce with one another, face a strange dilemma in the case of the polar bear. Polar bears are clearly different from grizzlies – they look different, eat different foods, remain active all winter and normally avoid grizzlies. But polar bears and grizzlies are clearly capable not only of mating with each another but of producing fertile offspring. That suggests they should really be considered only two subspecies of a single, common species.

Such crosses have always been rare in nature. Lately, however, grizzly bears have been expanding their range toward the Arctic coast, where polar bears are increasingly shorebound while waiting for sea ice to form. Sightings of "pizzlies," as some have proposed naming the hybrids, may yet become a common event.

THREATS TO POLAR BEARS

1. Global warming

The world's atmosphere is warming as we continue to pump it full of carbon dioxide, chlorofluorocarbons and other greenhouse gases. During the last decades of the twentieth century, global warming was the subject of scientific debate. There is no longer, however, any scientific question. The results of climate change are everywhere to be seen, particularly in the Arctic.

Melting permafrost, changes in ocean pack ice and starving polar bears were among the changes predicted by twentieth-century scientists in their computer models of future effects of climate change. Oil and coal interests tried everything they could to discredit the scientists and dismiss their predictions – but the predicted future has arrived. All across the North, permafrost is melting, pack ice is shrinking and polar bears are in trouble.

According to the US National Snow & Ice Data Center, winter ice covers less than fourteen million square kilometres of the Arctic Ocean today. Polar bears used to have access to a lot more frozen ocean surface than that; as recently as the 1970s, almost seventy million square kilometres of ice formed each year.

There is growing concern that the ongoing reduction in ice cover will create a positive feedback loop leading to even more rapid losses. Ice reflects sunlight, but open water absorbs it. As water temperatures rise in response to more sun exposure, the rate at which the remaining ice thaws could accelerate.

If that weren't enough of a problem for polar bears that rely on pack ice for hunting, sea ice is now forming later each fall and melting earlier the following summer. The ice-free period has been increasing at an average rate of half a day each year. This reduces the amount of time polar bears can spend hunting offshore and increases the likelihood of desperately hungry bears getting into trouble around human camps and communities.

Andrew Derocher, one of the world's leading authorities on polar bears, found that adult bears lose up to a kilogram of body weight for each day they spend waiting on the coastline for pack ice to form. Pregnant females lose even more weight when forced to fast – more than 4.5 kilograms a day. In a study published in 2004,

Derocher and his colleagues calculated that, based on measured trends in both pack ice formation and polar bear weight loss, by 2012 the average female polar bear might be in such poor condition that she wouldn't be able to produce cubs. Fortunately, the changes in ice coverage are not consistent across the whole Arctic, nor from year to year. Although many bears were showing severe stress by 2012, the fast slide toward extinction for the polar bear had yet to begin.

It may, however, be imminent.

Human lifestyle choices contribute directly to global climate change. The more energy we consume – directly or indirectly – the more oil, gas or coal must be burned to produce it. Burning fossil fuels increases the amount of carbon dioxide in the atmosphere. Carbon dioxide, like greenhouse glass, lets in light from the sun but holds back radiant heat that would otherwise dissipate into space. When we put more carbon dioxide into the air, we make this greenhouse effect that much more pronounced.

A carbon tax would be a powerful economic incentive to industry and consumers to cut down on the burning of fossil fuels that contribute most of the greenhouse gases causing the problem. Some governments and industries with a vested interest in promoting the development and sale of energy resources aggressively fight any consideration of such a solution, instead preferring to increase the rate at which they exploit dwindling hydrocarbon reserves. Increasingly, as the most accessible oil and gas get used up, the greenhouse emissions from new sources like Alberta's tar sands are increasing because of how much energy is needed simply to get them to market.

Until Canada and other governments get serious about reining in the reckless exploitation of our remaining supplies of hydrocarbon fuels, the prognosis for polar bears, and many other northern species, is not good. That won't happen until enough people demand it. Environmental citizenship at the individual level counts – as voters, we can choose political parties that promote carbon reduction measures; as consumers, we can choose to reduce the energy costs of our purchasing decisions.

2. Poison on the wind

Many toxic chemicals used as pesticides and herbicides in agriculture, or produced as by-products of industrial processes, are highly volatile. Once they evaporate, they become part of the air until they are deposited on land.

Scientists studying polar bears in the 1970s were shocked at high levels of PCBs, dioxins and other man-made chemicals in polar bear fat. Subsequently we have learned that global weather systems actually concentrate airborne pollution at high latitudes. There, it is taken up by plants and sea life, which are eaten by northern animals. Polar bears, being the top predators in the Arctic, concentrate the pollution in their body tissues. The chemicals contaminating polar bear fat have been shown to cause cancer and other diseases and to reduce fertility in studies of other species.

This problem will persist and grow worse as long as western society tolerates the release of synthetic chemicals – some of which are so different from anything that occurs naturally that they may never be broken down by microbes or other agents of decay – into the environment.

3. Egos

In the 1980s, people from many parts of the world became obsessed with adventure travel. The more extreme and demanding, the better. Several expeditions were launched to reach the North Pole or travel across the Arctic or trace the routes of earlier explorers.

Polar bears are curious, and they don't often see people out in the barren windswept expanses of the polar icepack. Børge Ousland, writing about a Norwegian polar expedition in 1991, described killing a curious polar bear that approached his camp. A few years later another expedition killed four polar bears. As southerners continue to invade the Arctic, more bears will likely die.

Churchill: polar bear capital of the world

Churchill, Manitoba – one of the most northerly seaports in North America – sometimes seems to have as many polar bears as people.

Polar bears waiting for the pack ice to form frequently wander through town. When they find food or garbage, they can become aggressive. Some bears have even preyed on humans. Churchill's innovative solution: it incarcerates habituated bears in pens in a large warehouse. When the sea ice is frozen it lets the bears out.

Once considered a nuisance, Churchill's seasonal gathering of polar bears has turned into a valuable tourism resource. People fly into Churchill from all over the world to watch bears. Many travel by "tundra buggies" – large-wheeled school buses that bump along unimproved trails across the subarctic tundra.

Hundreds of visitors to Churchill now pump millions of dollars into northern Manitoba's economy. Churchill was one of the early poster children for ecotourism. Some tundra buggy operators, however, travel far off of approved roads to get close to bears and allow their clients to feed candies or other junk food to polar bears and to harass bears to get better photos.

Nonetheless, Churchill, once one of the world's "black holes" for polar bears, now has a huge economic stake in keeping them alive. And the largest carnivore in the North has thousands of new friends.

Wapusk

Canada's thirty-seventh national park was formally announced in April 1996. The 11,475-square-kilometre Wapusk National Park is one of the largest parks ever established in Canada. It covers much of the Hudson Bay watershed between the Nelson and Churchill Rivers. Acclaimed for the important role it will play in the conservation of caribou, breeding and migratory birdlife, and historical remains, the park's name reveals one of its main attractions. *Wapusk* is a Cree word meaning "polar bear." The park is the result of cooperative planning efforts involving First Nations and the local, provincial and federal governments.

8
STUDYING BEARS

Two researchers were radio-tracking a large male grizzly in Yellowstone National Park's Hayden Valley one July day in 1984. One of the men stopped occasionally to hold aloft an H-shaped antenna and sweep it slowly in an arc to pick up the steady beeping of the transmitter on the bear's radio collar.

The beeping grew suddenly fainter as the men picked their way through heavy timber. Generally, the fainter the beeping, the more distant the bear. But in this case the bear had bedded down behind a large deadfall that muted the signal. As Doug Dunbar and Jim Hayden stepped around the tree, the three-hundred-kilogram grizzly exploded into a full charge.

Hayden leaped aside. Dunbar sprayed the bear twice with capsicum-based bear spray, momentarily disorienting the animal. Then it got its bearings and piled onto him, knocking him onto his back and biting at his belly. Dunbar had the presence of mind to spray the bear one more time, full in the face; this time the bear released him and fled.

The Yellowstone encounter was the first time bear spray had ever been tried in a field situation. It saved the lives of both a human researcher and a wild bear. The incident also highlighted the risks involved in radio-telemetry studies of wild bears.

Two grizzlies forage in tall grass.

John and Frank Craighead perfected the use of radio-telemetry for bear research in the 1960s. The Craigheads, working with national park rangers, captured grizzly bears at Yellowstone garbage dumps and fitted them with ear tags, other markings and, as they perfected the technology, radio collars. Early radio collars suffered from battery failures and a more basic problem – since bears undergo great changes in body mass throughout the year, a collar that fits today may simply slide off the neck tomorrow.

Radio-telemetry was a significant advance for researchers trying to track animals as elusive and wide-ranging as bears. Even so, the technique posed other challenges. Bears have mauled or even killed researchers trying to fit them with radio collars, a process that requires the capture, tranquilizing and handling of large, highly stressed animals. And bears occasionally die, sometimes from overdoses or accidents while recovering from tranquilizer drugs, sometimes for other reasons.

Wildlife officers had to kill two bears after a pre-construction study for BC's Coquihalla Highway. The bears' radio collars, fitted too tightly by inexperienced researchers, were slowly choking the bears to death. When conservation officers trapped an old male grizzly that was killing livestock in southwest Alberta in the late 1980s, they found a similar situation. The bear was sick and emaciated because of an old radio collar too small for its neck.

Nonetheless, radio-telemetry studies provided valuable information for bear managers and conservationists during the latter years of the twentieth century. Much of our basic understanding about the home range sizes, movements and food habits of black and grizzly bears came from radio-collared bears.

Modern radio collars are lighter and better designed than the early prototypes. When combined with long-life batteries and data loggers that capture exact locations from Global Positioning System satellites, radio-telemetry studies remain important in providing real-time location information on how bears travel through the landscape. Gordon Stenhouse, whose radio-telemetry grizzly bear research in the Foothills Model Forest was one of North America's most comprehensive studies of how bears cope with logging and other industrial changes to landscape, even experimented with mounting digital cameras on radio collars so that researchers could actually "see" what bears were looking at during their travels. The resulting insights simply aren't possible without radio-collared bears.

Even so, Stenhouse points out, capturing and collaring bears is stressful for the bear and dangerous to both bear and researcher. He and other bear researchers have been developing newer, less intrusive techniques such as DNA hair-snagging and the use of motion-activated cameras, to explore questions that radio-telemetry research left unanswered, and to do it in ways that minimize stress and risk for bear and researcher alike. Stenhouse's research team has even used chemical techniques to analyze bear hair for evidence of stress – akin to taking the pulse of a bear without the animal ever knowing.

With continuing advances in less invasive research techniques, there is less and less reason to put bears through the trauma of capture and handling by researchers. Data-mining – reanalysis of data from earlier studies in light of new questions or new statistical analysis tools – is another way that researchers can continue to add to scientific understanding of bears without subjecting them to bad experiences with humans.

How many bears?

The World Wildlife Fund estimates North America's black bear population at around five hundred thousand, with maybe three hundred thousand of those in Canada. Hunters kill less than 1 per cent of that number each year.

The problem is that those population numbers are almost meaningless.

The public demands numbers, so wildlife agencies provide numbers. But no wildlife agency in North America actually counts black bears in a consistent or reliable way. Most either provide best-guess estimates or extrapolate population densities from local, short-term bear studies to much larger and more diverse areas. Some biologists describe this, appropriately, as "mystery math."

Nobody knows how many black bears live in North America, and it's unlikely that anybody ever will.

Grizzly population estimates are better, because the agencies have put much more effort into counting them. Threatened and endangered species get more attention, and the wildlife agencies need facts to help mediate controversial debates between environmental groups who want better protection for grizzlies and hunting groups who want to preserve hunting opportunities.

Labour-intensive and expensive, the best numbers come from carefully designed DNA hair-snagging studies. Researcher Kate Kendall set out barbed-wire hair traps baited with strong-scented attractants in a seven-kilometre-by-seven-kilometre grid pattern throughout the range of the Northern Continental Divide Ecosystem (NCDE) grizzly population. Each bear that visited one of the scent stations left a sample of its DNA behind in hairs snagged by the barbed wire.

By 2004 her research team determined that at least 765 grizzlies ranged through this area in northern Montana and adjacent parts of BC and Alberta. Prior to Kendall's study, management agencies had estimated the population at less than half that number.

Fifteen researchers from the various agencies that manage the NCDE grizzlies or their habitats subsequently collaborated on a follow-up study. They tracked between thirteen and forty-two radio-collared female grizzlies each year from 2004 through 2009 to determine their reproductive rates and the survival rates of both the mothers and their young. Their final report, in 2011, relied on computer modelling to estimate that the NCDE population had grown about 3 per cent annually to at least one thousand bears.

DNA studies in Alberta, on the other hand, stirred up controversy when the provincial government's finger-in-the-air political estimate of their grizzly population turned out to be grossly inflated. Alberta politicians and hunting groups had long asserted that the province had more than one thousand grizzlies. But once Gordon Stenhouse and other bear experts had evaluated the numbers from a series of DNA hair capture studies and then subjected their findings to a lengthy peer review, the final population estimate came in at fewer than seven hundred bears.

Ironically, since bear counts are usually instigated to resolve controversy, the release of a new population estimate always generates a new debate. The government accepted the best-available-science population estimate when it finally declared the grizzly a threatened species in Alberta. But bear hunters who want the grizzly hunting season reinstated promptly turned to junk science in hopes of producing a higher population estimate. Determined to prove the scientists wrong, a Grande Cache-based outfitters group is tallying up anecdotal sighting information from hunters across the province.

Scientific bear-counting exercises can provide important and valuable baseline information, but they are too expensive and time-consuming to have much value in tracking population trends from year to year. Biologists keeping track of how bears respond to management decisions usually rely on simpler index measurements, like how much potential habitat bears actually use, what percentage of female bears are producing cubs or how many bears die unnatural deaths each year.

STUDIES OF BASIC BEAR ECOLOGY

Investigations into the food habits and habitat use of bears in various settings are the basic stuff of bear ecology studies, and grist for numerous master's theses in universities across North America. Over the years, young researchers have pursued radio-collared bears through the forests and wetlands of virtually every national park in North America at one time or another. Such studies usually last two or three years, too short a

A tagged bear snacks on dandelions.

time to develop a comprehensive understanding of bear ecology but long enough to develop intelligent questions and the beginnings of answers.

Longer-term study programs are rare and usually initiated by a crisis. One such crisis was the classification of the grizzly bear as an endangered species in the US. The need for scientific information to help the species recover led to establishment of the Interagency Grizzly Bear Committee (IGBC) which has overseen decades of research in Wyoming, Montana and Idaho. When two young students died in one night in two separate grizzly attacks in Montana's Glacier National Park, it led to almost a decade of research funding.

A real understanding of bear ecology requires

long-term studies that last at least five years. One reason is that bears reproduce slowly and their populations respond slowly to environmental changes. Another is that bears can show entirely different patterns of landscape use and food choices from one year to the next, in response to variations in weather that influence the distribution of food on the landscape.

The Craigheads' research in Yellowstone, subsequent investigations by the IGBC's Interagency Bear Study Team and the two-decade-long grizzly habitat studies that Gordon Stenhouse has overseen for Alberta's Foothills Research Institute are among the few examples of such long-term research. Although Canada's national parks conduct no long-term studies, Parks Canada ecologists have built an impressive long-term understanding of bears through monitoring programs and adaptive management.

RESEARCH TO REDUCE CONFLICT WITH HUMANS

Scientists can usually get find funding for studies that help protect economic interests from bear damage. Some of their findings have helped bears, too. Bears that raided commercial beehives used to be shot on sight – some still are – but research into the use of electric fencing proved that inexpensive and more proactive alternatives were possible. Other research has helped reduce the impact of black bears on sapling trees in commercial forest plantations by demonstrating that this damage was associated with a short period in the spring when bears need food energy but other food sources are scarce. Based on the research, some forest companies simply put out feeding stations to distract the bears until after the spring flush of sap is over and other natural foods have become available.

Charles Jonkel's students at the University of Montana conducted tests on captive bears to find an effective deterrent to help people avoid bear attacks. Their research resulted in the wide availability, today, of bear-repellent pepper sprays.

Valuable bear research doesn't even always require researchers to interact with bears. Stephen Herrero conducted extensive interviews with living victims of bear attacks. He also revisited the sites of past maulings to develop a better understanding of the factors that lead to bear attacks and influence their outcomes. His resulting book – *Bear Attacks: Their Causes and Avoidance* – makes sometimes gruesome reading but has been widely hailed for helping reduce the risks of visiting bear country.

Bear seasoning

Research at the University of Montana has shown that capsicum (pepper) sprays are superior to sprays derived from skunk musk and vastly better than mace. Mace, in fact, enrages bears and can lead to more aggressive behaviour.

Charles Jonkel and his students started researching bear deterrents in 1981. Using caged problem bears that had been provided by wildlife officers, researchers provoked them to attack and then sprayed them to assess their response. In another study, researchers put food baits out at a dump used heavily by black bears, and then sprayed black bears that approached the baits.

A 10 per cent concentration of capsicum was found to work in virtually every case. The usual response of sprayed bears was to immediately stop, turn and run away, often stopping to paw at their faces before continuing to retreat. Even more significantly, researchers found that bears that had experienced the spray were much less likely to charge subsequently.

Based on the encouraging early results, U of M researchers decided to see if pepper sprays could be used to "reprogram" problem grizzlies. In the past, the only option for aggressive grizzlies with a strong affinity for human foods was to kill them. Thirteen problem black and grizzly bears were used in the first experiment. Every time one of the bears approached a human or human-scented object, they were blasted with pepper spray. When the bears had learned to associate the painful spray with all things human, they were released into the wild. Only one of those bears returned to its old ways and was subsequently killed.

Based on this research, rangers in Denali and other US national parks were soon using capsicum to reprogram problem bears. The rangers deliberately recreated the conditions under which those bears had previously gotten access to human food or garbage, and then sprayed them with capsicum or shot them with rubber bullets. Stephen Herrero believes that this negative conditioning has saved bears' lives and possibly human lives too.

Bear sprays have been on the market for many years now, and there is no question that they work; several incidents have now been documented where the spray turned away a charging bear. A review by the US Fish & Wildlife Service concluded that bear spray is better protection than a gun. Subsequent research by Herrero and researchers from Utah State University confirmed those findings: if you want insurance against aggressive bears, leave the gun at home and hang a can of bear spray on your belt.

CONSERVATION BIOLOGY RESEARCH AND MODELLING

Perhaps the biggest challenge facing any bear biologist trying to understand or account for the ways in which bears go about their lives is the sheer complexity of natural ecosystems. Landscapes are mosaics of many vegetation types, landforms and microclimates. Bears use a wide variety of food sources, and bear populations depend on things invisible to human observers, such as genetic diversity, breeding cycles and mortality rates.

Conservation biology developed in the late twentieth century as an integrated discipline that pulls together research on populations and landscapes. Conservation biologists work with recent technological advances to find answers to questions of survival. How many bears are enough to ensure that a population will retain all of its genetic diversity in the future? How much of the landscape can bears actually use? How do human land use decisions affect the quality of a bear's life?

Geographic information systems (GIS) harness the power of computers to store and manipulate immense amounts of data in order to recognize patterns and produce analyses. Conservation biologists build huge computer files containing layers of spatial information on vegetation, soils, slope, aspect, snow duration and other

265

habitat variables. The computer is then put to work analyzing all these parameters, conducting millions of calculations in a few seconds and generating analyses some of the early bear biologists could never have imagined possible.

In Banff National Park, ecosystem scientist Cliff White correlated bear and landscape data with information on human use intensities to develop predictions about the interactions between bears and tourists. His analysis became a key tool in Parks Canada's decision to remove some development from places where it was blocking bears from important travel routes.

Conservation biology based on GIS modelling has proven the need for corridors of secure habitat to help bears move through the landscape. It has shown the impact of roads and clear-cuts in reducing the security of bear habitat, and the degree to which human recreational use of national parks affects the ability of bears to travel and forage safely. The map-plotting capabilities of GIS systems enable researchers to produce three-dimensional maps and graphics that show how bears and landscapes interact. Bears benefit not just from the research and analysis but from improved science communications that support better-informed decisions.

NON-INVASIVE STUDIES

DNA is the biological blueprint for each individual in the world. Every one of our cells contains it. Bear DNA is very different from human DNA, so for many years it has been relatively easy to tell one species from another by traces of DNA extracted from blood or tissue. Continuing advances, however, now make it possible to differentiate between two individuals of the same species, often from very small samples. One of the first times the public became widely aware of DNA analysis was during the sensational media coverage that followed the murder trial of US football star O.J. Simpson; today it has become an overused plot device in many television crime series.

DNA analysis makes it possible to identify not only an individual bear but also its relationship to others in the population. Mike Gibeau analyzed the genetic makeup of grizzly bears in and around Banff National Park, using these recent techniques. He looked for similarities in the DNA of different individual bears. The results showed most of the bears seem to be closely related, an indication that few are breeding and there is little crossbreeding with bears from other areas. That information played a big part in the Canadian government's decision to invest many millions of dollars in the massive overpass structures that now eliminate what was previously a barrier isolating bears on either side of the highway.

Using a mix of high-tech genetic analysis and low-tech barbed wire, bear researchers across western North America have conducted intensive population surveys that enable far more accurate estimates of grizzly numbers than ever before. The researchers set out scent stations baited with fish oil and ringed with a low-slung single strand of new barbed wire. Visiting bears leave tufts of hair, complete with DNA-rich hair follicles, on the barbed wire.

Some researchers have also experimented with stapling barbed wire to bear rub trees, so that visiting bears contribute hair samples while scratching their backs and leaving scent messages for one another. In

Banff National Park, however, camera monitoring of these sites showed that even non-intrusive techniques can change bear behaviour. Up to half the bears that visited rub trees simply avoided rubbing on the ones with barbed wire attached, with the strongest aversion being shown by mothers with cubs.

The cameras that detected this response are another example of recent, non-intrusive monitoring techniques. Advances in military and surveillance technology have made it possible for researchers to hide cameras beside trails, at wildlife communication trees or near den sites, collecting images that offer insights into bear numbers, behaviour and interactions with other species. The cameras are motion-activated, and many have invisible infrared flashes so that they will take pictures any time an animal passes, day or night.

Getting the real poop on bears

Bear droppings have always been a useful source of information about the foods that bears eat. More recently, biologists have found another use for them.

The same DNA analysis techniques that allow identification of individual bears from their hair follicles may work on mucus from fresh bear droppings. Biologists in Sweden have had good success identifying individual bears from the DNA they excrete, but according to Gordon Stenhouse the technique has yet to prove itself in North America.

Bear research may lose some of its romantic appeal for young biologists if pooper-scoopers rather than telemetry receivers become its new standard.

More than just bears

The motion-triggered cameras that Alberta-based wild-life biologist Cam McTavish pointed at bear rub trees were meant to answer questions about how many different bears were using Yoho National Park's Odaray Plateau. But, as often happens in research, the images also raised intriguing new questions about the entire wildlife community.

"Paul Paquet and I started up at Lake O'Hara region in 1990 or so. We were monitoring bears because of some bear incidents that had happened right on that one little plateau up there. We made these little jury-rigged camera systems with ammo boxes, and pop bottles glued to the front of instamatic cameras with pieces of junk hot-glued on the back, and we threw them up on some bear rub trees since that seemed the best way to catch images of bears and be able to tell them apart.

"And sure enough, we were getting bears rubbing on bear trees. But mountain goats would move by too and you could see them diverge to actually contact these rub trees. On close inspection, I found goat hairs on these bear rub trees. Then, over the five-year period I worked up there, we saw just more and more species touching these trees and dwelling around them, and it just became clear that these weren't just bear trees.

"Something more was going on, but just what could that be?"

As remote camera technology improved, McTavish expanded his studies of what he had once thought of as bear trees. He has now captured images of mule and white-tailed deer, moose, elk, bighorn sheep, wolves, wolverines, martens, squirrels, wood rats and porcupines using the same trees. Some mark the trees with

A grizzly and a wolf mark the same wildlife tree.

urine or by rubbing against it. Others appear only to be "reading" the information on the trees with their noses. But one way or the other, the whole wildlife community seems to use many of these trees to pass on or to collect information.

Carnivores seem to be the most active users of these wildlife communication trees. McTavish and Mike Gibeau found, for instance, that more than 80 per cent of all the wolf scats along park trails were near rub trees.

Just how complex is this communications system centred on what used to be thought of only as bear trees? Researchers have barely begun to consider the question. In the meantime, McTavish is concerned that thoughtless removal of some trees could have big impacts on the animals who use them to exchange information.

"This system has evolved over many years, it's way more complex than we're able to understand yet, and it's obviously functional on their level. So to mess with it by forest clearing or fires, I think that's a real issue.

"I've been thinking a lot about the value of these animal communication trees. If we could understand the possible value of these sites ... you know, we're talking about one kind of phenomenon here, bear rub trees or whatever you want to call them. But maybe this type of thing is happening on a whole variety of different levels and we just have not even begun to put our finger on any of that."

9
BEAR-WATCHING

WHERE TO GO, WHEN TO GO

Finding a bear used to be as easy as a trip to the nearest park garbage dump. Nowadays, garbage is no longer available to bears in most national parks; it's stored in bear-proof containers, trucked to enclosed transfer stations and then hauled to centralized landfills.

National parks and the larger provincial parks remain the best places to watch bears, but now you have to find them on their own turf, where they live like real bears rather than garbage-pickers.

The key to finding bears is to focus on habitat they are likely to use during the season when you are looking for them. Watch for bears at dawn and dusk when they are most likely to be actively moving around. Park information centres generally provide weekly or daily updates of recent bear sightings, so checking in with information staff can pay off.

The best time of year to look for bears in most areas is early spring – late April and May. At this time of year, the high country is often still covered with snow, and the most advanced green vegetation is at low elevations and in open areas. Bears and other wildlife are easy to spot because most of the trees and shrubs in bear

An explosive situation: photographers
crowd a female grizzly with cubs.

country don't leaf out until late May. Added advantages at this season: roads have little traffic, accommodation is more available than later in the year, and the odds are better that you can enjoy an undisturbed view of the bear without attracting a bear jam.

Another good time to look for bears is from mid-August through early October, when they again congregate at lower elevations to feed on ripe berries. Their visibility may be lower at this season, however, since the foliage is dense and a bear can spend a long time buried in one clump of berry bushes without exhausting the berry supply. Traffic is heavier in parks during early fall than in the spring.

Some recommended places for bear-watching in western Canada:

Canadian National Parks   www.pc.gc.ca

Banff National Park
403 762-1550
Icefields Parkway near Bow Summit: Grizzly bears forage in the open subalpine meadows along the Icefields Parkway in May and June. In summer it's worth glassing the timberline country and avalanche slopes along both sides of the valley, especially early in the morning.

Waterfowl Lakes area: Black bears are often seen along the Icefields Parkway eating dandelions in May and early June. They also forage in open areas and forest edges around the lakes.

Cascade and Spray River valleys: The wilderness backcountry of Banff's Rocky Mountain Front Ranges is important grizzly bear habitat. The bears use avalanche paths, stream floodplains and formerly burned forests that have not yet filled in with mature pines. Some areas are seasonally closed to hiking and horse travel, to protect grizzlies from human disturbance and reduce the chances of a human/bear confrontation.

Yoho National Park
250 343-6783
Mount Dennis: Bears are sometimes seen on the north side of the Ottertail Flats, across the Kicking Horse River from the Trans-Canada Highway. Grizzlies may occasionally seen digging roots and browsing in the open avalanche paths just west of the town of Field; the best place to search for them is from the parking lot of the park information centre, using binoculars. The best season is spring, but in summer they can also be seen at high elevations.

Kootenay National Park
250 347-9505
Marble Canyon/Paint Pots area: Late April to early May and again in October are the best times for glassing the open avalanche slope meadows on the west side of the Vermilion River valley. Grizzlies and the occasional black bear use these open habitats for root digging and browsing on low vegetation.

Hector Gorge/Kootenay Pond area: The young pine forests along both sides of the highway are full of fallen logs, legacy of a fire that swept the Kootenay Crossing area decades ago. Black bears find ants and grubs in the decaying logs, buffalo berries in the understorey of the pine forest and dandelions and other vegetation along the highway and in the numerous open hollows and wetlands throughout the area. Any time of year is good for spotting black bears early in the morning, but early spring is best.

Jasper National Park
403 852-6176

Maligne Valley: watch for black bears and occasionally grizzlies right along the road in April, May and early June. Use binoculars or a spotting scope to glass for grizzlies on the open green slopes overlooking Maligne Lake, especially in April and May or again in October and early November. The same slopes often hold big-horn sheep and mountain goats.

Icefields Parkway: black and grizzly bears feed along the highway right-of-way from April through June; black bears concentrate on dandelions while grizzlies dig sweetvetch roots and graze young grasses. Even in summer this is a good place for an early morning or late evening drive. Watch not just the roadside clearings but also the open meadows and forest edges along the floodplains of the Athabasca and Sunwapta Rivers, where, if you don't see bears, you might be lucky and spot a caribou.

Edith Cavell Road and Highway 93A north of Wabasso Campground: black bears are regularly seen near the road here, with spring again being the most productive time.

Waterton Lakes National Park
403 859-2224

Cameron Lake: The avalanche slopes at the south end of the lake – part of which are actually in the United States – are important seasonal grizzly bear habitat. Grizzlies are best spotted by glassing across the lake from the parking area very early in the morning. Spring is the best season, but spells of hot sunny weather during the summer can produce bear sightings too.

Red Rock Parkway: Black bears and the occasional grizzlies are frequently seen along the entire length of this road. Watch the open slopes north of the parkway, as well as the meadows scattered along Blakiston Creek. Bear sightings increase in mid-August during years when the abundant saskatoons along the lower part of the valley produce lots of fruit.

Sofa Mountain and Mount Vimy: With a good pair of binoculars or a spotting scope, you can frequently glimpse grizzly bears or their tracks early in the spring. Glass from Waterton Village, the Linnet Lake area or the Chief Mountain Highway.

Mount Revelstoke and Glacier National Parks
604 837-7500
Rogers Pass: Early spring is the best season to spot black bears along the highway edges or grizzlies foraging on the open avalanche slopes above the highway.

Pacific Rim National Park
604 726-7721
Some local boat tour operators offer trips to watch black bears along beaches in the Clayoquot Sound area.

Riding Mountain National Park (Manitoba)
204 848-7275

Prince Albert National Park (Saskatchewan)
306 663-5322

Kluane National Park (Yukon)
Phone   403 634-2251

Alberta Provincial Parks
www.albertaparks.ca

Peter Lougheed Provincial Park
403 591-7226
Highwood Pass: Grizzlies are common sights in this high-elevation pass, which transects a complex of avalanche slopes, old-growth forests and open grassy slopes. These habitats are particularly valuable to grizzlies during snowmelt in the spring, and again in late fall when the bears eat buffalo berries along the forest edges or dig roots on open slopes.

British Columbia Provincial Parks
www.env.gov.bc.ca/bcparks

Mount Robson Provincial Park
250 565-6759
Yellowhead Highway (Hwy 16) and Kinney Lake Road: In late April through early June, black bears are often feeding on the rights-of-way.

Bowron Lake Provincial Park
778 373-6107
Bowron River: Both grizzlies and black bears use the area; best time to watch for them is September, during the salmon run. There have been several dangerous encounters between canoeists and bears in recent years, however, and some bear biologists are now

recommending that the Bowron canoe route be closed during the spawning runs.

Tweedsmuir Provincial Park
250 397-2523
Atnarko River: There are limited opportunities to spot bears in September and October, during salmon spawning runs.

White Grizzly (Goat Range) Provincial Park
604 358-2333
Whitewater Glacier Trail: Excellent viewing opportunities for grizzlies, including rare white-phase ones. Foot access only; travel with caution.

Tatshenshini–Alsek Provincial Park
250 387-2928
Haines Road: Grizzlies are regularly seen in open habitats between Pleasant Camp and the Yukon boundary. Commercial rafting tours are available, providing excellent opportunities to view grizzlies in spectacular wilderness surroundings.

Khutzeymateen Grizzly Bear Sanctuary
No public access, but professional guides are available to take parties into this protected area in late spring, when grizzlies congregate on tidal flats to feed on sedges. Bear viewing tours are available through:

    Ecosummer   1 800 465-8884
    Ocean Light II   604 328-5339
    SunChaser   604 624-5472

United States National Parks   www.nps.gov

ALASKA
http://dnr.alaska.gov/parks
www.nps.gov/state/ak

Denali National Park
907 683-2294
Access to the core of this park is available by public transit only. Grizzlies and other wildlife are highly visible in the open subarctic landscape.

Kodiak National Wildlife Refuge
888 408-3514
Almost seven thousand square kilometres on Kodiak Island were set aside for bears, salmon and other wildlife in 1941.

McNeil River State Game Sanctuary and Refuge
907 267-2253
Congregations of as many as fifty or more grizzlies feed on summer-spawning salmon at a series of waterfalls – North America's largest concentration of grizzlies. Visitor numbers are strictly regulated to protect bears and humans. Prospective visitors must apply in a lottery, and around 250 are selected. Ten go in at a time, with a biologist/guide, to look at bears that have become highly habituated to the close presence of humans.

Katmai National Park
907 246-3305
West of the McNeil River Sanctuary, this area also supports large numbers of bears which fish for salmon in

July. Access to the area is not controlled by lottery, but there are very strict rules of behaviour to ensure that bears and humans are safe.

MONTANA

Glacier National Park
406 888-7800

WYOMING

Yellowstone National Park
307 344-7381

HOW TO WATCH BEARS

1. Show respect

Stay well back from the bear and give it plenty of space. Never give a bear any reason to feel threatened or nervous. Allow the bear to choose how close it wants to be to you. The golden rule applies here: behave toward the bear the way you would like the bear to behave toward you.

2. Stay safe

If you are watching a bear from the road, pull your car well out of the line of traffic and park before concentrating on the bear; many vehicle accidents happen because of people forgetting the rules of the road when seeing a bear. Always remain in or beside your vehicle in case the behaviour of less responsible people triggers an aggressive response by the bear.

3. Invest in good binoculars, a telephoto lens and/or a spotting scope

Tools that help you enjoy a good view of a bear from a distance will help you resist the temptation to put your safety, and the bear's survival, at risk.

4. Never try to influence a bear's behaviour

Feeding bears, whistling or shouting at them, trying to herd them into a better position for a photograph and other forms of deliberate harassment are not only dangerous and disrespectful, they are illegal in most national and provincial parks. A bear that is able to behave naturally near humans is a rare and valuable creature – don't let your behaviour spoil it.

5. Leave early

If a crowd is starting to gather or the bear's behaviour seems to be influenced by your presence or the location is unsafe, just leave. If you see a mother grizzly with cubs, just leave. The good news is that the bear is there and you are alive and well. Self-discipline and restraint are valuable virtues in bear country. Nobody wants to have to live with unnecessary regrets. Once you've had a brief look, move on.

6. Do you really need that photo?

Cameras turn three-dimensional, living bears into two-dimensional images. They also tempt their owners to move in closer so as to fill the frame better. But there are lots of great bear photos available already. Why not use a notebook instead? Record details of the bear's behaviour, what it was eating, the nature of the habitat and other details. Writing observations down is a powerful way to learn the details of nature and stimulate insight; taking pictures, on the other hand, actually reduces your ability to observe detail and concentrates your brain on the camera rather than on the living bear in front of you.

7. Report problems

Park officials often welcome information about bear sightings. It's also important to let park or wildlife authorities know about any suspicious-looking behaviour on the part of humans. If you suspect illegal activity, use your notebook to record the details (time, licence plate numbers, description of suspects, their behaviour, other possible witnesses). Do not intervene. Humans can be a lot more dangerous than bears.

POACHER HOT LINES:
BC   1 800 663-9453
Alberta   1 800 642-3800
Saskatchewan   1 800 667-7561
Alaska   1 800 478-3377
Oregon   1 800 452-7888
Montana   1 800 847-6668
Idaho   1 800 632-5999
Washington   1 800 477-6224

Bear sprays

Capsicum-based sprays are classed as a restricted weapon in Canada. Possession is legal, but only for self-defence in the event of an animal attack.

Travellers crossing the Canada–US border in either direction can expect to have their bear sprays seized by customs officers (they can be picked up upon your return). However, you can still buy and own bear spray at your destination, so long as the product is clearly marked as being for use against animals.

Almost all outdoors suppliers in and near bear country stock legal bear sprays.

10
CONSERVATION RESOURCES

CONSERVATION ORGANIZATIONS

Organizations that buy or protect critical habitat

The Nature Conservancy of Canada
www.natureconservancy.ca
36 Eglinton Avenue West, Suite 400
Toronto, Ontario
M4R 1A1

Vital Ground Foundation
www.vitalground.org
Building T-2, Fort Missoula Road
Missoula, Montana
59804
USA

National organizations that promote wilderness or habitat conservation

Canadian Parks and Wilderness Society
www.cpaws.org
425 78th Avenue SW
Calgary, Alberta
T2V 5K5

World Wildlife Fund Canada
www.wwf.ca
245 Eglinton Avenue East, Suite 410
Toronto, Ontario
M4P 3J1

Canadian Nature Federation
www.naturecanada.ca
75 Albert Street, Suite 300
Ottawa, Ontario
K1P 5E7

Canadian Wildlife Federation
www.cwf-fcf.org
350 Michael Cowpland Drive
Kanata, Ontario
K2M 2W1

ECOTOURISM AND BEAR EDUCATION

Alberta

WildSmart
www.wildsmart.ca

The Jasper Institute
www.friendsofjasper.com

Waterton Natural History Association
www.wnha.ca

British Columbia

Get Bear Smart Society
www.bearsmart.com

Montana

The Great Bear Foundation
www.greatbear.org

Glacier Institute
www.glacierinstitute.org

Wyoming

The Yellowstone Association Institute
www.yellowstoneassociation.org/institute

FURTHER READING

Brown, Gary. *The Bear Almanac, 2nd Edition: A Comprehensive Guide to the Bears of the World.* Guilford, Conn.: Lyons Press, 2009.

Gailus, Jeff. *The Grizzly Manifesto.* Calgary: Rocky Mountain Books, 2010.

Herrero, Stephen. *Bear Attacks: Their Causes and Avoidance.* New York: Lyons & Burford, 1985.

Hummel, Monte, Sherry Pettigrew and Robert Bateman. *Wild Hunters: Predators in Peril.* Toronto: Key Porter Books, 1991.

Masterson, Linda. *Living with Bears: A Practical Guide to Bear Country*. Masonville, Colo.: PixyJack Press, 2006.

Petersen, David. *Ghost Grizzlies: Does the Great Bear Still Haunt Colorado?* Durango, Colo.: Raven's Eye Press, 2009.

Russell, Andy. *Grizzly Country*. New York: Lyons Press, 1967.

Russell, Charlie. *Spirit Bear*. Toronto: Key Porter, 1994.

Russell, Charlie, and Maureen Enns. *Grizzly Heart: Living without Fear Among the Brown Bears of Kamchatka*. With Fred Stenson. Toronto: Random House of Canada, 2002.

Thomas, Debbie, and Maureen Enns. *Grizzly Kingdom: An Artist's Encounter*. Calgary: Detselig Enterprises, 1995.

Wilson, E.O. *The Future of Life*. New York: Knopf, 2002.

Woodcock, George. *Peoples of the Coast*. Edmonton: Hurtig, 1977.

AFTERWORD

One July afternoon, I joined a small group of campers for a guided hike with a park naturalist in Waterton Lakes National Park. It was warm day. An occasional junco trilled sleepily in the forest along Lineham Trail, and the distant sound of cascading waters rose and fell on the down-valley breeze.

We had crossed a grassy avalanche slope and re-entered the pine forest when our guide, Vincent, stopped the group and turned to talk to us. His eyes were on my face when they suddenly focused past me and widened. "There's a bear!" he said.

We turned. Twenty metres away, an old grizzly was plodding up the trail behind us, seemingly lost in a daydream. I remember being struck by the sag of her paunch and the way her lips flapped as she walked. It felt vaguely unreal to see her so near, in the bright light of day and so seemingly oblivious to our presence.

Vincent and I held our arms high and shouted, trying to make sure she would see us before she got near enough to feel threatened by us. The rest of the group stared, spellbound.

The bear stopped and looked at us. She half-turned, then looked back again. Clearly she didn't want to change her plans even if we were blocking the trail. She hesitated, evidently weighing her options. Then she stepped off the trail and continued walking toward us through the trees. She never deigned to glance at our group as she passed, maybe two metres away, and disappeared around a corner.

Suddenly a chorus of children's screams and shouts erupted.

I popped the clip from my can of bear spray and jogged up the trail, expecting the worst. But before I had run more than a few steps, two little girls appeared, followed by two more, then two more – a whole procession of bug-eyed, white-faced little twelve-year-olds. They were now singing at the tops of their lungs under the firm direction of four equally disconcerted teenage counsellors.

As the first children passed, one looked up with eyes like saucers, extended her arms and said, "There was a bear only *this* far away from me!"

The singing and chatter of young voices faded down-valley. The wind eddied among the trees. Again we could hear the far rush of newborn waters and the faint sounds of birds foraging in the shadows.

Vincent and I called an end to the hike and escorted our excited companions back to the trailhead, talking about bear safety and past encounters and all the things people talk about when they are still pumped up with adrenalin, suddenly bonded together by a sense of shared danger.

No doubt the little girls had good stories for their parents next time they phoned or wrote home. No doubt their parents told their friends about the close calls their daughters had had, just as Vincent's and my hiking companions went home with a grizzly encounter to boast about.

But what had happened, really?

A bear had tried to walk up Lineham Creek valley and found the valley full of people. That's all.

Finding herself in a stressful situation, the bear

figured out a solution to it and went on with her life. All the fear, adrenalin, excitement and frightful possibilities had been created in the minds of the people involved. If circumstances had been different – if the encounter had taken place outside the protection of a park, perhaps – somebody might well have shot that bear and the story would be retold again and again of their narrow escape. Probably after a few iterations, the bear would have evolved into a raging, foaming-mouthed killer.

That's what we do to bears. While it remains true that bears are capable of attacking and killing people, it remains no less true that they almost always choose not to ... and that in our dealings with bears we too often focus on our fears and fantasies, not on their reality.

The most dangerous thing about a bear is not its claws, teeth or disposition; it's how we react to it. When we behave as if they're tame pets, harmless clowns or dangerous killers, we create the situations that lead to danger. We may survive those situations. The bears usually don't.

Bears and humans can share our increasingly crowded world safely. But for that to happen, we need to learn to respect bears for what they really are, and to see that the choices we make almost always affect bears and other wildlife.

Bears have few choices: they need habitat, they cannot compensate for unnatural mortality, they must forage opportunistically for food and they are bound to act aggressively when they perceive an imminent threat to their young or a valuable food source.

Humans are similar to bears in some ways – we share, for instance, long life, intelligence, omnivorous habits and a capacity for doing harm to other creatures

– but we differ in that we humans are both blessed and cursed with imagination, we have many choices and we are capable of ethical restraint. We are capable of fear – but we are also capable of managing our fear by learning to understand and respect our fellow beings.

Past human choices have brought us to a time when almost every bear species in the world is under threat. The choices we make tomorrow – about resource development, roads, agriculture and tourism, as well about our own personal behaviour in bear country – will determine the future of the dwindling bear populations that survive today. If those choices are informed by ethical restraint – and by informed respect rather than fear – then bears may have a future.

Kevin Van Tighem has studied wildlife and their habitats in western Canada for almost 40 years. He long ago lost count of how many bears he has encountered and observed in the wild. A naturalist and hunter, he has written more than 200 articles, stories and essays on conservation and wildlife which have garnered him many awards, including Western Magazine Awards, Outdoor Writers of Canada book and magazine awards and the Journey Award for Fiction. He has served on the executive committees of the Federation of Alberta Naturalists, Alberta Wilderness Association and Foothills Model Forest. His decades of work in landscape ecology, conservation biology and nature interpretation in the national parks of western Canada culminated in 2011 with his retirement as superintendent of Banff National Park. Kevin currently lives and writes in Canmore, Alberta.